ADOPTION:
More Than
By Chance

Beth Kozan

Adoption:
More Than By Chance

To Marie —
Happy Reading!
Beth Kozan

Side By Side Publishers
Phoenix, AZ

Visit online booksellers
Cover art by: ArtGirl-Annie Holman
Cover design by: Eduardo Cerviño

ISBN-9781508584988

Dedication

This book is dedicated to the many foster home and receiving home parents I worked with, in Tucson and metro Phoenix, Arizona. Their unsung devotion to the babies and toddlers they kept for hours, days or months while important decisions were made -- are appreciated.

Table of Contents

Part Five: All Grown Up –

Adult Adoptee Stories **109**

Part Six: Miracles and Near-Miracles **145**

Introduction

Sal and Debbie were shopping for their nephew's Easter basket when I called them at home. The message I left on their answering machine (pre-cell phones) said to call me as soon as they got in. I would tell them they'd been chosen for a baby boy already born, and the birth mother had signed her adoption papers. Tomorrow, they would take their baby home.

Debbie told me later that while they were in the checkout line, she wanted to buy a blue Grover Beanie Baby from a display near the register. "Don't jinx getting a baby by starting to buy toys!" Sal admonished her. Debbie reluctantly placed the stuffed toy back on the shelf. When they got home, they returned my call. I was so happy to end their wait for a baby to adopt.

The next morning, they came to the agency's office to learn about their baby's birth mother and to pick up their baby boy. The birth mother's worker told them why she chose them to be her baby's parents: she liked that they had dated since high school, and that cars played a big role in their meeting – when Sal drove his hot rod past the drive-in restaurant where Debbie and her girlfriends were parked. With each circle around the drag, they flirted a little more and soon they were dating. The worker also told the new parents that the mother would like to meet them in a few weeks, once she and they were used to their new roles. Sal and Debbie quickly agreed.

Then it was time to meet the baby! The foster mom brought the baby to the room in a carseat, and – aside from being delighted with the baby – Sal and Debbie looked at each other in amazement. There in the carrier next to the baby was a blue Grover Beanie Baby that was the birth mother's gift to the baby. It was just like the one Debbie had wanted to buy the night before. Sal and Debbie will tell their son someday how they knew this was a sign that he was the child meant for them.

This book is a collection of stories about connections in adoptions – connections that seem 'more than by chance.' Stronger than mere coincidence, these stories from all angles of adoption have brought me to believe there are no accidents, and that the phenomenon of synchronicity validates the stories people tell about their adoptions. I am honored to have witnessed this process in many adoption placements.

Some Adoption Definitions

Like all specialties, adoption has its own language, and a basic vocabulary is necessary to understand adoption practice today. To be clear: adoption is a process that establishes a legal relationship of parent-to-child for a child born to one set of parents and raised by a different parental figure(s).

Over the years, a common language in the field of adoption has evolved: indeed, it is always evolving. In the five years since I retired from adoption agency work, the preferred terms for adoptee and birth parent have changed!

At the center of the discussion is the adopted person, the one who has been adopted (preferred by adopted people over the word 'adoptee' which diminishes the person to a state of never growing up). The adopted person has two sets of parents: the first parents (also called 'birth parents') whose genetic material combined to make the adopted person, and who nurtured the child for the prenatal period or longer, and the adoptive parents who become the legal parents by a court process thereby taking on the duties and responsibilities of parenthood.

Most of my experience has been in voluntary placements in which a pregnant woman (often a single mother) works though a decision to have another parent or set of parents raise the child. This woman does not become a birth parent until she signs papers to activate the decision of adoption. Most voluntary placements (also known as private placements) are handled by adoption professionals such as agency social workers, attorneys, facilitators or specialists in adoption. Private placements are funded by a combination of charitable contributions and fees paid by adoptive parents. There are also involuntary placements where the child has been removed by a court process, almost certainly because of abuse or neglect or abandonment. The fees charged in such public placements are quite low (if fees are charged at all) because the costs are covered by tax dollars we all pay. A publicly-funded agency, such as the State's Department of Human Services or a County Adoptions Unit, assists with these public placements.

Decision counseling is the process by which a pregnant or parenting client (most often the mother) looks at the options and decides to choose parenting or plan an adoption. The world outside of adoption often defines that choice as between keeping a baby or giving it away. Changing the wording to reflect the reality of that choice influences the birth mother's pride in the decision-making process. Additionally, the adopted person who learns that it was a reasoned decision is better prepared for self-acceptance than one who believes he was given away, sight unseen.

Similarly, adoptive parents have taught us the insensitivity in such commonly used phrases as "real parents" and "natural parents" when used instead of birth parents, because that implies that adoptive parents are unreal or unnatural. Now, the preferred term is gradually changing to "first parents" as some people think birth-mother denigrates the original family to merely the act of birthing.

The most recent opposing philosophies in adoption pertain to open adoption versus closed adoption. Open adoption (as used in this book) refers to the placement of a child when the birth family and the adoptive family share identifying information (addresses, phone numbers and email addresses) and have direct contact with each other. An agency or facilitator might have brought them together initially on a first name basis, but bows out once everyone feels comfortable with direct contact.

A semi-open adoption (for our purposes here) refers to an adoption where the birth family and adoptive family know each other by first names and use a third party to arrange meetings and to facilitate contact through letters or meetings.

A closed adoption (also called "traditional adoption") grew out of a social system that sought to protect everyone by establishing secrecy as the main concern for an adoption.

There are many problems with closed adoptions and many challenges with open adoptions. Most successful adoptions today are a combination of these approaches, meaning they may start off as closed or semi-open and grow over months or years to become fully open adoptions.

Moving Toward Open Adoption

"You tell me they love him," said one birth mom in my office thirty years ago, "but how do I know they love him?" The next day the adoptive mom was in the office. "Is she doing all right? Has she changed her mind? Does she want him back?" The fear of the unknown was tearing each woman apart. If they could meet each other, I reasoned, they would like each other; instead, they are afraid.

Alas, in those days the law kept us from following the instinct to bring these two women together. Gradually the laws in most states have changed and we are allowed to let all sides of the adoption meet each other, but it has been a slow process.

The movement toward openness in adoption is rooted in the context of personal rights movements of the 1970s and 1980s. Women making adoption plans for their babies were less willing to be consoled by pacifying generalities like, the family who will adopt your child is a young professional couple married ten years who own their own house and have established careers. They can afford to give your baby all the things that you cannot.

Potential birth moms were empowered to ask direct questions: "What kind of 'professional'? What kind of house do they live in? A mansion? A condominium? Where do they live? In the city? In the country?"

So to answer those questions, we wrote descriptions of our waiting families, and labeled them Family A, Family B, Family C. This necessitated a code sheet to kept things straight when asked questions about the families. Then the families wanted to know what we'd written, thinking they should have a hand in their own descriptions, so we had them write their own letters of introduction. Gradually, they added photos of themselves and their activities.

The first time I showed a picture of her baby to a birth mother, it was for (I told myself) "therapeutic reasons." She was struggling to accept the plan she'd followed six weeks earlier. The baby girl, fathered by an African-American man, was very pale at birth, and when the Irish/Italian birth mother called her own father with the news that he was a grandfather, he reacted to the race issue just the way she had predicted: with bigotry.

Since then, however, and remembering the pale little face she'd loved in the hospital, she had tortured herself thinking she could have returned home with the baby and never told her father of the baby's bloodlines.

I knew, since the adoptive couple had left a photo at their last office visit with their adoption worker, that the little girl's complexion had darkened considerably and that there was no mistaking the child's African-American heritage. Telling her this could have seemed placating; she needed to see the portrait herself. I obtained permission from the reluctant adoptive mom to show the picture to the birth mother in my office. I can still see her face as the birth mother looked at the wallet-sized photo. It satisfied in her something deeper than the question of race.

"She looks happy," she said. "She is loved." I knew that the decision to share the photo had been the right one.

A few months later a different birth mom asked to have a picture of her son sent to her. "But if she sees how beautiful he is," objected the new father, "she'll want him back!" Perhaps she did, in part. But she also knew that by law, she couldn't get him back.

When she saw a photo of her nine-month-old son standing beside his toy box, she blurted out: "His legs work!" Gradually, birth mothers taught me that seeing pictures relieved their fear of the unknown.

Early pictures that adoptive parents sent to be shared with birth parents were often cut in weird shapes to exclude the other children at a birthday party or to eliminate the faces of relatives. An unidentifiable child in a Halloween costume was another favorite way to comply with early promises of pictures.

Over the years in our educational classes, as we've had prospective adoptive parents meet birth parents who have placed, the barriers have come down. Without the fear of the unknown, it's much easier for adoptive parents to understand that the genes their child carries are not to be feared and for the birth parents to see that the child is loved in his new home.

Today's adoption preparation should include mandatory classes where the prospective adoptive parents also meet adoptive couples who have open placements. The focus is on what's best for the child. When the atmosphere is one of respect, the children grow up more secure in themselves. As one of my waiting parents pointed out, "It doesn't have to be a competition; it can be a partnership!"

Before we started having adoptive parent education classes where birth parents spoke after their placements, adoptive parents could pretend that we just magically produced babies from "the baby closet" down the hall at the agency. Once they met real women and men who made the difficult decision to let someone else raise their child, a new respect was gained for the role of the birth parent. That can't help but grow a healthier adoptive person.

Healthier than someone who, at the age of twenty-five and with curly red hair, finally had an opportunity to read her background that she'd never known, and exclaim, "I really am Irish; all my life I've been asked if I am Irish, and I haven't known!"

Or healthier than the young man who looked up from reading about his birth parents who were college students at the time of his placement and said, "They sound pretty normal! I was braced to find out that they were skid row alcoholics or had psychiatric problems!" What a burden to carry around for years, when it was completely unnecessary!

Adoption Laws Shape Adoption Practice

Adoption in the United States is governed by state law. There are many things that differ from state to state: when and where the adoption paperwork (variously called 'consents,' 'surrenders' or 'relinquishments') can be done; the amount of money that can be paid by adopting parents and to whom; how the rights of the father are dealt with; the waiting time before the adoption becomes final – all of these can and do vary.

The law that governs how a placement is handled is usually the law of the state where the adoptive parents reside. There are a few states that allow non-residents to adopt in the state where the baby was born, but those are exceptions.

When a baby is born in one state but adopted in another, the Interstate Compact on Placement of Children comes into play. Each state has an ICPC Administrator that reviews the paperwork to be sure it meets the legal standards of the sending state (where the child is coming from) and the receiving state (where the adoption will be finalized). Adoptive parents must receive clearance from both states before they can take the child from the state of birth. Obtaining the clearance can take several days.

Another law that is important to know about is the Indian Child Welfare Act of 1978. If either birth parent is eligible for membership in a federally recognized Native American tribe, the adoption has to be granted under the Indian Child Welfare Act, known as ICWA. This requires a waiting period of ten days prior to consents being signed and they must be signed in front of a judge.

The judge asks the parent if they understand English; if not, a translator in their native language will be provided, and hearing then proceeds.

The adoption consents, the mother is told by the judge, can be rescinded at any time until the adoption is final or until the parental rights are terminated in court.

When the placement is involuntary (when the Indian child has been removed by the State due to abuse, neglect or abandonment) there is a placement priority written into the law. The first choice under ICWA is for placement within the same family; next choice is for placement with an extended family member; the third choice is with a family from the same tribe; fourth choice is with a family from another tribe; and the last choice is with a non-Indian family.

Eligibility for tribal membership varies from tribe to tribe. It may depend on blood quantum (the percentage of Indian heritage) or it may depend on having an ancestor whose name appears on a certain years' Tribal census.

All this attention, means that anyone involved in an adoption needs to have excellent legal representation and persons knowledgeable in adoption law specific to the states involved.

Stories of Synchronicity

In the thirty years I worked for adoption agencies, plus five years of private practice in adoption related counseling after retirement from agency work, I collected a lot of adoption stories. Many of them I told to help illustrate a point I was making, and to encourage others who were struggling or questioning the role adoption plays in their lives.

As I began collecting stories for a potential book, I noticed there were frequently stories of synchronicities involved. People would tell me their stories sometimes with incredulity in their voices; a sense of wonder.

I began to see books with titles like *There Are No Accidents*. Spirituality teachers spoke about synchronicities in Life. Carl Jung is thought to be the first person to identify the word, and likened the feeling of synchronicity as familiar as the feeling of déjà vu.

Once you identify and start to notice synchronicities, you see them more and more. I trimmed down the book of stories, mercilessly cutting to the meat: the heart of the matter.

And people tell me their stories of synchronicity, too. All the stories in this book I had a hand in, so to speak, and experienced the similarities along with my clients.

Sometimes there's a danger in telling stories that may engender expectations. What if you're adopted but you don't see synchronicities in your story? It doesn't invalidate anyone's story not to find eerie connections, but it also doesn't take long to find that all adoption stories are special!

PART 1

THE MATCH

The Match

When new applicants first turn to adoption, they tend toward two ends of the spectrum:

Some say they will take any child; that neither the gender, the race nor the age matters -- they just want a child to love. At the other end of the spectrum, there will be applicants who want a healthy newborn as much like them as possible, and as young as possible. By the time they go through the process of preparing for adoption (the home study, education classes, suggested readings), we expect both ends of that spectrum to have come more toward the middle.

If they say they are open to any ethnicity, have they thought it through from the child's viewpoint? Do they live in an ethnically diverse area? If not, are they willing to relocate for their child's sake?

We also hope those with narrow expectations in the beginning will open their hearts to other possibilities. Perhaps they will consider a child who is older than newborn, or maybe they'll be willing to discuss a child whose mother used street drugs. We help people explore their limits and arrive at a level of comfort that will be best for all concerned. Whenever possible, we try to place a child with a family of the same ethnicity. Therefore, we make special efforts to invite families of all cultures to adopt.

When we had panels of birth parents meet with prospective adoptive couples, the waiting ones always asked: Why did you pick the family you chose for your baby?

They hoped for a magic formula to write their introductory letters so they would be chosen. Birth mothers say there was one that 'stood out above the others.' It could be the smiles on the couple's faces, or it might be the dog in the picture. Once, it was piano in the background of a photo. "I always wanted to take piano lessons," sighed one young pregnant woman. "Now I know my baby will have that chance."

Some birth mothers have described a "glow" that lit up one family's profile and set it apart from the others. Some birth mothers can't put it into words except, "It was just a feeling; I just knew." Sometimes after the placement there is something that happens that lets us know "yes, this is it!"

The Trout Baby

Sixteen year old Julie was sure she was in love with Jeff, the baby's father, and pleaded with her mother, promising to make an adoption plan if only her mother would quit insisting she get an abortion. Her mother finally agreed and went to Catholic Social Service in Anchorage and asked if there was a place she could send Julie to have the baby. She learned about Merilac Lodge in Tucson, run by Catholic Community Service.

Although Julie had never been farther south than Seattle, she was soon flying to Arizona, and I met her at the airport. Julie was in the first trimester of her pregnancy when she got off the plane. She asked if coconuts grew on the palm trees at the Tucson airport. (They don't.)

In those days, we workers made the choice of what family got what baby. Julie had been brought up in nature. Her family had fished, camped out and gone hunting for all kinds of critters.

We had a waiting couple named Basil and Marti who had been waiting for over two years (which was a little longer than the usual wait then). They were avid outdoor sports enthusiasts. The photographs they'd submitted with their application reflected these interests. One photo, taken on a fishing trip, showed the husband holding a string of three fish and his wife leaning against a big boulder in the middle of a stream. I saw a faint resemblance in the facial features of the birth mom and the adoptive mom.

Julie's baby was the first I was to place after my supervisor retired. Until then, all the babies at our agency went into foster care upon discharge from the hospital. When the baby was at least seventy-two hours old, we would take written consents, and then call the family to tell them to come to the agency the next day to pick up the baby.

Julie didn't want her baby going into foster care, and I didn't see any reason why we had to do it just because it had always been done that way. I could make a placement as soon as the papers were signed. The only thing I needed to do was check on was Jeff's plans; he'd been strong about the adoption plan when I spoke with him by phone. Would he sign the papers as he had said he would?

The day the baby was born, I tried to reach Jeff by phone in Anchorage. His mother told me he'd gone hunting on the Kenai Peninsula for two weeks.

In the two conversations I'd had with him, he'd never indicated he might interfere with Julie's plan. I wanted to proceed with the placement, but could I take the chance he might decide to parent the baby?

At that time, all babies and moms were kept in the hospital for 72 hours. The night before Julie and the baby were to be discharged, Jeff called me. He'd returned early from his trip and got my message.

He sounded tense and nervous, so to put him at ease, I tried small talk: "What did you get on your hunting trip?"

"It rained the whole time we were out, and I didn't get anything but three rainbow trout." (I immediately thought of the picture of Basil and the fish in the file at the office.)

I told him his baby girl had been born and that I needed to know if he was still in agreement with Julie's plan of adoption. "I just don't want Julie to come home with the baby and think we're going to get married," he said. "I know I'm not ready to settle down and be a father."

At the office the next morning, I carried the picture of Basil around the office. "Do these look like trout?" I asked anyone who might know. "Do they look like rainbow trout?" They were! That was my first experience with the "pat on the head" that let me know this was the right placement for this baby.

There's more to this story. I kept those pictures on my bulletin board at work for a long time and frequently told the "Trout Baby" story. When Megan, for that became her name, was six, I saw the adoptive couple for the first time in years.

"I have a new picture for you," said Marti. "This summer we went fishing with another family. Out of two boatloads of people, no one caught anything but Megan. She caught three rainbow trout! I'll send a picture for your bulletin board." And she did.

Breast-feeding? Are You Sure?

Sam and Linda came to see me to make a permanent plan for their unborn baby. I learned that they had met at a Christian college and their friendship had developed more quickly than either of them had anticipated. Now they were afraid their relationship might not survive the stress of the unplanned pregnancy.

In the midst of their prayerful approach to their dilemma, they reasoned that if God wanted them to pursue the adoption route, He would lead them to the right family for the baby. They asked for a family that lived their lives by the Bible, who said grace before meals, and who regularly studied the Word of God.

This was long before we asked adoptive parents to write to birth parents, but I knew Marti and Basil well enough to ask them to compose a letter explaining their religious beliefs. I gave them no guidelines other than: "Just write something about your beliefs and your church."

Marti quickly sent a letter describing their church and their deeply held beliefs that showed God as an integral part of their day-to-day existence. When Linda and Sam read the letter, it was perfect. "The answer to our prayer!"

A day or two later, Marti called to ask what the reaction had been to her letter, and to ask when the baby was due. I replied that the baby was due within a week, but I needed to caution her about something. This young mother wanted to breast-feed her baby in the hospital. Doing so might make it even harder for her to part with the baby, but the mother wanted to give her child the best start in life she could.

Instead of reacting negatively, Marti immediately said, "That's great! I'm planning on breast-feeding, too. I wanted to know when the baby is due so I can get ready!"

Although I'd read that adoptive moms could breast-feed, I hadn't met anyone who had tried it. (It can be done either by the use of hormones to stimulate milk production, or by using an attachment that holds a supply of formula the baby feeds on while breast milk production is stimulated by the baby's nursing.) Marti said she had wanted to breast-feed their first baby, but the two-year wait for Megan was too anxiety-producing to keep up the preparation. When I told the birth parents of Marti's plan to breast-feed, they saw it as further evidence that this was a match meant to be.

A Chance Meeting

There was the time I was at a truck-stop in Casa Grande, Arizona, to take consents from a mostly Spanish-speaking birth couple. I needed a witness for the paperwork.

When I arrived, I recognized someone I hadn't expected, who was also having lunch at the restaurant: It was Chip, an adoptive father with whom I had placed two children several years earlier. I knew Chip spoke Spanish! He had worked in international banking where he'd met his wife; they were raising their children to be bi-lingual.

I asked Chip if he would act as witness and also speak with this young couple in their primary language. He was more than willing to do so. Because my Spanish is very poor, I don't know exactly what Chip said to them, but I could see tears in his eyes and relief in the faces of the birth parents.

I don't believe it was an accident that brought Chip to this restaurant at the time when he was needed to give peace to this young couple.

On A Trip to Korea

This evidence of a message was there, even with the first adoptive home study I completed; I just didn't have the experience at the time to recognize it.

They were the quintessential high school couple: Bob was quarterback of the football team; Sandy was the head cheerleader; they were homecoming king and queen. Their high school romance blossomed and they married half-way through college. Two boys within the first five years of marriage, and then they decided to try for a girl. Even if it turned out to be a boy, they vowed that would be their last try. Soon, Sandy was pregnant once again.

A modern husband, Bob volunteered to have a vasectomy while Sandy carried this, their last pregnancy, to term. Bob underwent surgery before the baby was to be born.

Bob was there for Sandy as their long-awaited baby girl made her appearance. She seemed perfect! However, in the nursery, tests done revealed their precious baby girl was born with a defective heart and wouldn't live long. Within a month, God took their little angel to live with Him.

A few years later, Bob and Sandy added their little girl by adopting a toddler from a Korean orphanage. Their two blond boys were so proud of their brown baby sister!

Bob's job in the expanding field of computers took him to the Far East a couple of times a year. On one trip, he arranged to visit the orphanage where his little girl had lived. He wanted to take pictures for his daughter, now nine years old and starting to ask the normal questions that an adoptee needs answers for, to understand where she came from.

Bob was welcomed by the orphanage director, who asked the purpose of his visit. "Well, to adopt another little girl, of course!" Bob replied in jest.

He was given a tour of the orphanage, plus the name of his daughter's native village and instructions so he could go there to take pictures. As he was preparing to leave, the director of the orphanage looked at him intently.

"Were you serious about wanting to adopt another child?" she asked. "Because I have a special little girl here who needs a home. As you know, we are licensed only for children up to the age of three. We have an eight year old who was brought here by her grandmother," she continued. "The girl has been acting as an aide to help with the babies, because legally she isn't supposed to be here."

She explained how this little girl came to the orphanage. At three years of age, she was scalded when she tried to lift a pot of hot water from the stove. Her arm was permanently scarred and as a result, she had been abandoned by her mother and left to be raised by the grandmother. By Korean custom at the time, the scar meant that she would not be "marriageable" when she grew up. She could only hope for the most menial of positions and might even face a life on the streets in order to survive. The grandmother had brought her to the orphanage and begged, "Get her an American family, a family who can let her grow up to be somebody." Then the grandmother left in tears.

That night at his hotel, Bob called Sandy and talked to her about the possibility of adding another girl to their family. She talked to the kids. Their sons were now teenagers and the daughter was nine. Could the boys stand another sister?

Was their daughter willing to share her room with a new sister who would be the same age and the same ethnicity?

The family vote was Yes! And together they decided to pursue adding this child to their family. I got to write their home study (my first!) and oversee the adoption, the first of many happy families I would watch overcome the obstacles of culture and language to become a family.

The Name is ?

Evelyn didn't intend to name her baby when she was born; she thought that was a choice that should be the parents who would raise her. This was in the days when moms who planned to have their babies adopted were discouraged from having any contact with their babies, in the belief that it was "easier" that way.

Hospital staffs take special care of the adoption babies, especially those who stay in the nursery rather than in the mother's rooms, and the nurses in the Tucson hospital would give the babies names to call them if the mothers hadn't.

The nurses called Evie's baby Sarah. When I told Evie that, she was relieved to know the baby wasn't a "no-name" in the hospital. She then, in her head, added the middle name to make her Sarah Elizabeth; this would be the name she and her family thereafter referred to when speaking of "the baby."

When I met with the adoption worker after placement (I worked only with the birth moms at that point in my career), she told me the family had chosen the name Elizabeth Sarah, which they had planned years ago as their girl's name. Sharing that piece of information with the birth mother let her feel it was meant to be, too.

Eyelashes

Baby Jonathan was born back when we workers were the ones who chose which family the baby would go to.

His new family lived in a distant small town, and Ella, the adoptive mother-to-be, was a teacher attending summer school at the University of Arizona in Tucson.

She and her husband didn't even know there was a baby on the horizon for them. Those were the days when all babies to be placed for adoption went into foster care for at least one day to give the time needed to take the mother's consents. Then we would call the adoptive family when the papers were signed and say, "Come to the office tomorrow to get your new baby!"

Of course, they would want to drive to the office immediately, but we would insist, "No, get plenty of sleep tonight and come see him tomorrow!" Rules were rules, even if they didn't make sense.

Ella had called me when she enrolled in summer school and told me her schedule.

I knew that the day we would call to say consents were signed would be the day before her final exams. I couldn't do that to her! So I called her husband Jim in their hometown 180 miles away. I told him I'd let him decide how to tell Ella that they could take their baby home, and he made an appointment for 2:30 PM, only hours after Ella's final exam.

The next afternoon, a breathless Ella and Jim arrived promptly at two-thirty. She was wearing a new T-shirt on which was printed: *Any woman can be a Mother – it takes someone special to be a Mommy.* Underneath had been added these words: "***At 2:30 P.M., July 12!***"

Jim told me how he called Ella the night before and told her he had to come to the city on business the next day and would meet her at the student union for a late breakfast after her exams. He knew she wouldn't eat before a big test!

When they met, he handed her a bag containing the T-shirt, which he'd bought at a custom T-shirt shop. She read it, murmured an embarrassed thank-you, sure that he was insensitive to her infertility. Then she screamed, "July 12th is today!" He told her they were going to the agency to pick up their baby boy!

After the finalization of their adoption six months later, we went to lunch. As we sat in the restaurant, I noticed that baby Jonathan and his adoptive mother share an unusual feature. Both of them have eyelashes that grow straight up from the lids with an extra curl. I recognized this unusual way for eyelashes to grow. And here they were, two biologically unrelated people, a mother and her adopted son; a little boy whose eyelashes grew just like hers.

Nails as Body Art

One of the checks that adoptive parents in Arizona have to pass is their fingerprint clearance. We became somewhat skilled at taking the fingerprints in our office.

When I prepared to roll the prints of Steve and Loretta, I was challenged by Loretta's long sculpted nails. It was difficult to flatten her fingers enough to get a clear image on the card because her nails were a good two inches longer than her fingers. A short woman with short fingers, Loretta worked to present the illusion of long graceful fingers by lengthening her nails. Although I'd seen longer nails a few times in my life, these were no doubt the longest nails I'd ever grappled with while fingerprinting.

We proceeded to study Steve and Loretta shortly after they submitted an inquiry because they were open to many different situations – racially mixed children, a child already born, drug use and other situations that not all prospective parents are accepting of. After fingerprinting and individual interviews, I made a home visit as the final step before writing their home study to send to the court.

We had just discussed "child desired," and I had taken notes to incorporate their parameters into my report. As I was preparing to leave, Loretta added, "And if you had a baby that needed to be in foster care while you looked for the birth father or for some other reason, we would be open to taking a placement like that." As I drove away, I mulled over this latest information.

Just the day before, I had met an expectant mother who was already past her due date. Brittany's baby would be half African-American and half Anglo. At home she was already caring for three children under the age of three: her son and daughter, and her new boyfriend's son. All three children were in diapers, and with visitation issues between the other parents; their plate was full.

The father of the baby she was carrying, however, was in another state and she didn't have a current address for him. I knew I was going to have to hire a private detective to locate him, serve him with a Notice to Potential Father, and wait thirty days to see if he responded. The baby, when it was born, would need to be in temporary care for at least thirty days, and we don't like to move a baby more times than necessary. Might Steve and Loretta's home be a proper placement as foster-adopt parents?

We had other waiting families that were open to a bi-racial baby, and the next day at the office I polled their workers to see how those prospective families matched Brittany's requests for a family for her baby.

Raised in a strong Catholic home, her first request had been for a Catholic family; none of the already approved families on the list who were open to a bi-racial placement were Catholic. I scheduled a talk with my supervisor to discuss a fost-adopt placement.

I was a little embarrassed to mention another factor in this match: the pregnant mom, like Loretta, wore her fingernails about two inches longer than her fingers! It was weird to consider a match based even partially on the length of fingernails, but it turned out to be the 'final nail' that hammered home the decision of which family Isaiah would grow up in!

Sturgis

When we first started doing face-to-face meetings, the naysayers predicted there would be birth parent situations that were "too scary" to present to prospective adoptive parents, who after all, were sometimes in a desperate, we'll-take-anything status; or conversely, so fearful of the unknown they would turn down anything not 'perfect.' After twelve years or so of doing adoptions where people didn't meet, I was of the belief that unseen and unknown situations are almost always harder to handle than reality.

My theory was put to test when a young teenager came to talk about placing her eight-month-old baby. She had been excited to be a mother at first, but the responsibility had set in. Now she wanted to go out and have fun. She was disappointed to learn that her mother, who'd had her kids as a teenager, didn't want to raise another baby. She didn't feel like a granny at thirty-five!

After several counseling sessions in which her options were explored, the young woman took home a few profiles for her family to read. They asked to meet Chad and Sandy, a new couple in our program. Their home study had been done by another agency and a different social worker – now on vacation – had done their intake interviews. I had met Chad and Sandy in education class, but I didn't know the details of their backgrounds.

The teen mother brought her mother and her mother's boyfriend to the introductory meeting. They were bikers who looked the part! Each had visible tattoos and long, flowing hair. Now I saw the young mother's extremely short hair as possible teen rebellion.

After nervous introductions, Chad said quietly, "We used to live in Sturgis."

"Wow, Man!" said the biker boyfriend. I didn't know what was going on, but I noticed an immediate release of tension and an acceptance on both sides. They patiently informed me (the outsider) that every summer motorcyclists come to tiny Sturgis, South Dakota where they have a motorcycle ralley.

I decided not to worry about birth parents choosing "the right family.

Baby Jared turned into a great kid. This early open adoption taught me a lot about trust – including trusting the Universe to find the right home for a child who needs one. Jared's new parents decorated his nursery with a Harley poster and his interest in wheeled vehicles continues. Sandy tells me they get together with Jared's birth family several times a year, usually at a park. Jared's even seen his grandpa's 'hawg.'

Horses

Some babies are not born in hospitals. Some babies are born *on the way to* the hospital.

One of our babies was born at the Avra Valley Fire Station north of Tucson. The mother lived in a rural area and was trying to get to the hospital in Tucson, but ended up delivering at the fire station.

The baby rated a perfect ten out of ten on the APGAR scale, a rating test given at one minute after delivery, and again at five minutes after delivery, and based on the baby's respiration, muscle tone, color, heart rate, and response to stimulation. The firefighters took the mom and new baby to the hospital in an ambulance. By that time I worked for an innovative agency in Scottsdale that ran television ads aimed at prospective birth parents. After seeing one of those ads on television while she was in the hospital, the mother gave us a call.

This woman in her mid twenties lived in the country and had horses. She's always been around horses. When she learned she could choose the adoptive family for her baby, she asked for a family with horses. We had a Phoenix family who had horses!

When we called the waiting adoptive family, we got their answering machine. We left a message to call the agency as soon as possible. Within a half hour, we received a breathless call. When we told the prospective mother that the birth mother wanted a family who rides horses, she replied, "That's why I wasn't home! I was at the stables, putting away my horse!"

Meant to Be

David and Eileen came to Catholic Social Service because they'd found a baby to adopt on their own. A connection through their church led to a young woman expecting a biracial baby who said she wanted to make an adoption plan. David and Eileen, both African-American, had been trying unsuccessfully to achieve a pregnancy, and a biracial baby would fit into their family constellation easily. They needed a home study done quickly, as the baby was due within a month. We began the study, and when the baby girl was born, David and Eileen traveled to Tucson where they met the birth mother in the hospital. The mother insisted the baby go home with them prior to the 72 hours that must pass before she could sign consents. They were so happy!

Two days later, their world fell apart when the mother, now overwhelmed with guilt, asked to have the baby returned to her. Her church family had rallied, taken up a collection and paid a month's rent for her so she could keep her baby.

There is no more wrenching task for an adoption worker than picking up a baby who has been in a prospective adoptive home and is being removed, no matter the reason. It is rare that this happens, but nevertheless, it is a painful thing to witness. I had that duty with David and Eileen. It is a helpless feeling for all.

David and Eileen did learn something valuable through this experience, however. They now knew for certain they could love a baby born to another mother. They had fallen in love instantly with this precious little girl. After a few days to regroup, they wanted to continue their adoption home study so they would be ready when the next opportunity arose.

It wasn't much longer before I had a call from a pregnant woman who was overdue and wanted to talk about making an adoption plan. Kaylee had broken up with her boyfriend, with whom she had two other children. As a single mother struggling to provide for her boys, she felt that adoption was the only plan that made sense. The baby would be three-fourths African-American. She had already called a few adoption resources in the phone book, and was turned down because they didn't have a family for her baby. Did I have a family? I immediately thought of David and Eileen, and gave a thumbnail description of them. Kaylee was relieved and we planned to meet the next week to discuss more details.

Over the weekend, however, Kaylee called me in a panic. Her mother was out shopping and her grandmother was sick. She had no way to get to the hospital, and she was in labor! I picked her up, and she begged me to stay with her. In only a couple of hours, a healthy baby boy was delivered, and Kaylee lovingly held him to her breast. Upon discharge, she decided to take the baby home so her boys could see their baby brother and she could breast-feed him. When the seventy-two hours were up, she would sign consents.

Because of their previous experience, I didn't want to tell David and Eileen about this possible placement until I knew it was certain that Kaylee would sign consents. Some breast-feeding moms *do* release their babies, but it does bond them to the baby and the baby to them, and I think it's harder to release the baby to adoption. Still, I believe entirely in self-determination, so if Kaylee needed to do it this way, I was in agreement. I called David and Eileen and asked how they were doing with their "Dear Birth Mother letter" I'd asked them to prepare. They almost had it done, and I urged them to get it ready.

Four days after the baby was born (not three) Kaylee called to tell me she was ready to carry through with her adoption plan. I took a witness with me, and we drove to Kaylee's apartment where she signed the adoption consents. We took pictures of her and all three of her boys. I gave her the letter and profile David and Eileen had prepared, complete with pictures of them.

When I got back to the agency, I called David and Eileen to tell them about their baby boy, and that the paperwork had been signed. What delighted screams I heard from the other end of the line! Eileen called David, and they went on a hurried shopping spree.

Two hours later I had a message they were in the lobby. Just as I started for the door, my pager went off – it was Kaylee's number. I returned the call and listened as a tearful and frantic Kaylee said, "I just found out that I know David! You have to tell them we know each other! Ask them if they still want to adopt my baby! I'm afraid they'll say *no!*"

After I had left her apartment, her boyfriend's mother had called to see how she was doing. Kaylee described David and Eileen from the papers I'd left, and it was then that she was reminded that she'd met David, her former boyfriend's work supervisor, once.

When I brought David and Eileen into my office, I told then of Kaylee's call. It was from David, then, that I learned that David had declined a meeting with Kaylee a few months earlier. It was right after they had lost the baby girl in the reclaim, and he hadn't even told Eileen about it; they were too deeply involved in their grief.

"I didn't want to get strung along again," David explained, especially when they were so raw from what had just happened. But under these circumstances, with the adoption paperwork already signed, there was safety in this placement. I left them alone to talk it over. It didn't take them long; they knew they wanted to adopt, and they felt fine with this situation. Jordan became their pride and joy. I don't remember ever seeing happier parents than David and Eileen.

Eileen wrote a book, *A Is For Adopted*, an alphabet book centered on the happiness of adoptive parents upon learning of their baby's arrival. With the colorful illustrations of Norma Strange, it is a welcome addition to the world of adoption books. Eileen and David and Norma are working on more letters of the alphabet *N is for No Smoking, Please!* is the second in the series.

A Message from an Earlier Time

One Friday in January, I received a call from a woman who told me her daughter Becky, who was now a freshman at the local university, had been adopted through the agency where I worked. She said they wanted to come in and talk to someone. Presuming that they wanted background information from her file, which at the time was stored off-site, I told her I would be happy to meet with them, but it would take at least two weeks to get any background information. "No," she replied, "that's not what we want to talk to you about. My daughter is pregnant, and she wants to talk about placing her baby for adoption through the agency where she was adopted!"

When they arrived, I learned that Becky had waited until late in her pregnancy before admitting to her parents (or to herself, for that matter) that she could be pregnant. Eight months earlier, Becky had been at a typical college party where there had been a lot of drinking. Things got out of hand. She didn't remember much of what happened, but the next day she realized she had been violated. As the months wore on, she admitted that she could be pregnant, and realized she had to tell someone. On one weekend trip home, she bravely revealed her predicament to her parents. When her mom started to get excited about a grandchild, Becky said, "No, Mom, I've been thinking of adoption. I've had such a good life with you and Pop that I think it's what I want to give my baby." They cried together, and then they talked about where to turn for help. Do you think we could go back to the same agency where I came from? It would be like repaying a debt," Becky said.

Still, it wasn't easy for Becky to make the plan for adoption. She struggled with her decision. One night she told her mom, "I wish I knew what my birth mother's advice would be. Do you think she was confused? What do you think she would say?"

Her mom swallowed hard and said, "Honey, there's something I have for you. I've always known there would come a time when I would know it would be right to give it to you. I think now is the time."

She went to the cedar chest and took out a special package. "When we picked you up at the agency, your birth mother had left this for you." She opened up a tiny bundle containing a little pink outfit and a baby blanket. "Your other mother wanted you to have this from her."

Holding these tangible items chosen especially for her, Becky said she felt her birth mother was telling her, "I, too, struggled with my decision. I, too, made a choice – a hard choice – but one made with love."

This was a very special blessing. Becky and her mom went to the store the next day and bought some purple material (Becky's favorite color) and set about to sew a matching outfit and blanket for her baby to go home in. Becky felt her two moms giving her support in her time of need.

PART 2

WAITING

Waiting

One of the hardest things for adoptive parents to do is to *wait.*

They've researched their infertility, attempted to solve non-parenthood by following their physician's directions only to experience disappointment, then struggled to arrive at the decision to adopt, and then they find they have to wait – sometimes for quite a lengthy time.

Doing all the things that adoption requires takes time. They have to be fingerprinted, share intimate financial details, bare their souls to social workers with the power to approve or deny their dream of family, attend required classes or read recommended books in order to complete the home study, and in Arizona, wait for the Court to approve the home study, all pre-placement. Waiting to receive a child can be very difficult.

The hardest waits are for the first child. Unsure of themselves in so many ways, waiting for a child that is wanted so badly can cause all kinds of feelings to jump up unexpectedly: anger, resentment, sadness, hurt. All these feelings come rushing forth to replace the feeling of joy that they most want to experience. Being in a supportive group while waiting can be helpful for couples, but it can also bring sadness. Someone has to be the first in the waiting group to get a child and someone has to be the last. Here are the stories of some of the "lasts" I have known.

Group Support

It was the mid-1980s. Our office had moved to a new location and there wasn't a room big enough at the new location to hold training sessions. We would have to find a church or a business with a free room where we could hold training classes. I mentioned this dilemma while on a home visit with a young couple who had called for information.

I normally would have met them at my office, but the turmoil of the move caused me to schedule a home visit. While we talked about how adoption works, it became evident they weren't quite ready to give up 'doctoring' in an effort to produce a baby. It might have worked. I don't know, for I never heard from them again.

During our meeting, however, as I discussed required classes and my dilemma of finding a meeting room, the husband asked how many people attend these classes. When I replied that with eight to ten couples, plus the panel presenters, we need room for twenty people at a time.

He suggested that the adoption educations classes be held in the homes of the families. "Our living room would hold about twenty people, more if we put chairs in the dining room," he noted. I looked around and decided, "Why not?"

Therefore the next few sets of adoption education classes were held in the homes of the participants. I often joke at any first meeting of adoptive parents by voicing aloud the question on their minds: "Who owns the big car in the parking lot?" "Who is the Competition?" "Who will get a baby before we do?" What we learned by having the meetings in their homes was that such concerns quickly dissipated and that everyone began to pull together for each other.

They shared their stories and they shared their contacts. We taught them how to network to find a baby for themselves. If someone got a call about a situation that wasn't right for them, they would share the resource with the other members of the group.

Each meeting was centered on a topic and we'd often have a speaker or a panel discussion. The members of the class had homework assignments such as reading a particular book or writing a letter to the baby they wished for. The group would then discuss these while the panel was preparing for their presentation.

After the program, staff and panelists would leave, and the families would stay.

Baby showers for new placements grew out of these groups, and often they continued to meet to celebrate birthdays of their children. Many of them still stay in touch now that their kids are adolescents.

In any group, the first family to receive a baby was often a surprise to all of us. Neither staff nor families had any idea who would be the first. Sometimes it was the least wealthy, or the quietest. Sometimes it was the couple we predicted would wait the longest because they were so specific about what they wanted.

The placement time might range over a year or even longer before a group of six couples would all get their babies. The next-to-the-last couple was so in tune with the issue of being last that the new mom often called the last waiting mom and apologized for getting a baby.

A Sure Thing

When we start a new education group of prospective adoptive parents, everyone wonders who will be the first family to get a placement. We tell them that usually (but not always) the first new parents in this group will be those who are an ethnically mixed couple, or who are open to ethnically mixed babies. It's not that we have more of those babies to place, but that we have fewer potential homes for those babies. In one of our groups, Ann and Lonnie were presumed to be an "early-match" because they were a racially mixed couple. Little did we know it would take over a year for them to get their 'forever baby,' and that they would be the last in their group to achieve a permanent placement.

The unpleasant side of adoption that everyone dreads is the baby who goes home with a family only to be reclaimed by the birth parents. Ann and Lonnie experienced such a placement not long after completing their education classes. Ann heard through a friend that another agency in our city was looking for a home for a racially mixed child. Ann and Lonnie seemed like the perfect match. Ann and Lonnie were scheduled to meet the prospective birth parents at the other agency the day I returned from vacation, and I went along for support. The birth father didn't come as planned, but the agency worker assured us that the adoption had been the birth father's idea, and that he supported the plan and would sign consents.

A couple of weeks later, the birth mother delivered a healthy baby girl and Ann visited her in the hospital. Lonnie was on a business trip out of town when the baby arrived, and the baby went to a receiving home until the seventy-two hours had elapsed and the birth parents could sign legal consents under Arizona law. The agreed-upon plan was that the birth parents would travel together to sign their consents, visit the baby at the agency, and Ann would take the baby home. Lonnie, who was out of state in his car, would be home in two days.

An option that was considered was to have the baby wait in the receiving home until Lonnie arrived, but everyone involved – the birth mother, the workers and Ann – thought the baby needed to be in her permanent home as soon as possible. The afternoon of the consent signing, the birth father called to say he'd had car trouble and would come to the agency the next morning to sign his papers. Since the birth mother was already at the agency, and so was Ann, we proceeded with the placement as planned.

The following morning, the birth father surprised everyone when he walked into the other agency with his sister and said, "Now that she's signed away her rights, I'll take the baby home." It was time to panic.

Since 1998, Arizona law has required us to serve the prospective birth father (when he is not married to the mother) a "Notice to Potential Birth Father." This gives the father thirty days in which to activate his parental rights. If he does nothing (as is often the case) the adoption can proceed without him.

Because this man had appeared cooperative from the beginning, he wasn't served; therefore, his thirty days had not been running. He was quickly served notice the next day, starting his thirty-day clock. We could do nothing but wait to see what his response would be.

One option that was available was to put the baby back into the receiving home during the wait. Lonnie had not yet met the baby. I encouraged them to at least wait till Lonnie was home, and then they could make the decision together. They decided to keep the baby in their home while they waited out the birth father's thirty days. Understandably, Ann and Lonnie were under stress.

We waited. And we waited. We checked the court docket electronically. Lonnie went to the clerk's office himself to check the docket daily, and he was the one to discover that on the twenty-eighth day, there had been a paternity action filed by the birth father. Attorneys for both agencies and the adoptive parents called a hasty meeting with Ann and Lonnie.

The birth father had successfully fought for custody of a five-year-old child that the State had taken just two years earlier. The advice of the attorneys was to return the baby. Sadly, thirty days after they took this baby home, Ann and Lonnie returned her to the other agency so the birth mother could take this child to raise. Under the law, once there was no adoption plan, her consents were no longer valid, and the child could be returned to her. The birth father promised the birth mother he would help raise the baby, and he was now satisfied with the decision.

This first disappointment was the closest Ann and Lonnie came to a placement for a year. Next they were matched with Angie, who was living in a homeless shelter. She said she wanted a stable life for her biracial baby. But when it came time to sign the papers, Angie couldn't make this difficult decision. The baby stayed in an interim home until Angie could get out of the shelter (where babies weren't allowed), find a job, and move into a homeless shelter that allowed moms with babies to live there.

Then one of the attorneys who had witnessed Ann and Lonnie's reclaimed baby called with a possible placement of a biracial child. That mom decided to parent without meeting Ann and Lonnie.

Later, there was a birth mom whose first match had fallen through when the family she picked saw a picture of the birth father and they realized that "Arabian" in this case meant a man with a dark complexion. At their face-to-face meeting, the pregnant client begged Ann and Lonnie to say they would take her baby. But when the baby arrived she decided with her family's support to keep the baby and raise him.

By that time, Ann and Lonnie were understandably feeling burned out, and so they directed their energies in other directions. They chose to further their careers by completing additional credits for their work.

The staff of our sister agency in Tucson would call when they heard about a biracial baby that might be available. All the other couples in their group, one by one, would ask their workers if Ann and Lonnie had a placement yet. Sadly, the answer continued to be *no*.

We got an unsolicited letter in the mail from an agency in Louisiana that needed a home for a baby girl in care. Both parents were African-American, and both had signed adoption surrenders in their state. There were no drugs or alcohol in the baby's or mother's past. The birth parents were both gainfully employed, and the mother was raising a child on her own and finding it difficult to do.

She was raised as an only child, with no father in the family, and her mother had recently died. The baby girl was healthy, and she needed a home. I called the agency in Louisiana to see if this baby girl was still available. She was. I told the worker of Ann and Lonnie's plight and then I sent by overnight mail their profile and home study to Louisiana.

A week later, I got a call from the worker in Louisiana. The birth mother, who had signed consents earlier, had been scheduled to come in to choose the family. She missed two appointments, and when contacted by her worker said, "It's too hard. I trust you to find the right family."

The workers had met and decided which of twelve possible families would be the most appropriate; they chose Ann and Lonnie. We started the paperwork through Interstate Compact, obtaining clearance prior to their leaving, so they could travel to Louisiana to meet their new daughter.

This time, there were no hidden problems.

One of the other workers and I went to the airport to meet Ann and Lonnie and Baby Lauryn when they arrived from Louisiana. This was a homecoming we were more than happy to participate in!

The plane was late, and we waited patiently. In this time before the TSA and the resulting airport security issues, we were able to wait for the arrivals and mix with passengers waiting to board the plane. They were headed to the plane's next destination: San Diego.

When the plane headed to the gate, two little boys started jumping up and down. "It's the Shamu plane!" they cried. Southwest Airlines paints some of its planes in themes that honor their hub cities. The plane Ann and Lonnie and Baby Lauryn had boarded in New Orleans had started the day in Orlando, and was headed for San Diego.

We met Ann and Lonnie with an "It's a Girl!" balloon, and helped them (and all their stuff) to the shuttle that would take them to their car.

Back at the office, I pulled their letter to remove it from the stack of waiting parent profiles. In one of their pictures attached to the letter, a photo I'd forgotten showed Ann and Lonnie at an earlier vacation spot: with a person dressed as Shamu, at San Diego's Sea World. If I needed it, here was another sign this was 'meant to be'!

Shapes

Karen has a poetic soul. During the home study, she told me about a poem she wrote incorporating her feelings about her infertility, the uncertainty of the wait for a baby, and the ultimate acceptance that there would be a baby for her in her future. In her poem, she wrote about the trees that line our city streets, and how they hang over the street in a box shape.

In fact I, too, had wondered when the city crews found time to trim the trees so that the trucks that pass by would not be whipped by the overhanging branches.

As Karen explained in her poem, it is the traffic that shapes the trees. Karen noted that she, like those trees, was buffeted about by life's trials and tribulations and, like the trees, she was shaped by her experience.

Karen's husband Mark worked for one of the airlines at the airport. Karen was eager to quit her government job as soon as they got their baby. As time went by and others in their group got placements, they were afraid no birth mother would choose them. Shortly after Christmas, however, there was a baby meant for them!

When the baby arrived for placement, I sat with Nancy, the devoted receiving home mother who had kept the baby while the birth mom made her decision. In another room, the adoption worker was giving Mark and Karen their baby's background.

When he had learned of the birth mother's older children at home, Mark had brought a gift for them – an inflatable model airplane representing the airline for which he worked. It could be hung from the ceiling or given a hands-on workout, and would provide hours of imagination for her boys.

It was a cold day, and Nancy had wrapped the baby in a warm blanket. I loosened the blanket and lifted the baby out of the car seat.

One of the joys Nancy gets from loving the babies she keeps is that she chooses their placement clothing. She dresses each baby girl in the sweetest, frilliest, seasonally appropriate dress, and finds boy clothes for the little fellows.

Nancy had found an appropriate outfit for this baby without knowing where the new dad worked. The light blue sleeper was covered with yellow airplanes! "How did you know?" I started to ask. But of course, she didn't know. It was more than by chance!

Without Group Support

What is the longest I've known a couple to wait for a baby? I think the longest was the couple in Tucson who waited six years for number two. Warren was nearing the end of his career in the Air Force. They had received their first child, J.R., while Warren was stationed at Davis-Monthan Air Force Base near Tucson.

When they were ready for number two, Warren got a transfer to an airbase in Utah. They were there for two years, and Carole Anne would call periodically to let us know they could fly to Tucson at a moment's notice. For some reason, though, we were going through a dry spell. There were comparatively few babies placed for adoption during those particular years.

Finally, they moved back to Tucson, Warren retired, and I got to know them a little better. They had worked for J.R.'s placement with the worker who trained me at ACHA who had retired.

I visited them when J.R. was about seven. Later, Carole Ann told me that as she was putting J.R. to bed that night, she explained why I had come to visit them: it was because I was going to help them adopt a new baby.

This naturally led to a retelling of his own adoption story, after which J.R. asked, "Do you know my birth mother's name?" Carole Ann told him she did not. "I think I know her name," said J.R. shyly. "You do?" asked a startled Carole Ann. "I think her name is Beth!" Carole Ann called me the next day to tell me. I was flattered.

For many years on the Sunday before Thanksgiving, and as part of National Adoption Month of November, Arizona Children's Home in Tucson (now they've changed their name to Arizona's Children Association) held an Adoption Celebration. Warren and Carole Ann were one of the couples that worked to make these events a success. After I moved to Phoenix, I liked to travel back to attend the Adoption Celebration to see "my kids," who were growing older.

One year I got to see J.R.'s little sister, the child who was worth the six-year wait. She was about eight then. Over punch and cookies, Carole Ann told me that her daughter had decided that after she graduates from high school she wants to go to Germany.

I was stunned. We did so little sharing of personal information back in the days when her daughter was placed, could Carole Ann have known?

Her birth mother, after placing this child for adoption, took off for a six-week tour of Europe with her best friend. They had Eurail passes and visited Germany, Switzerland, France and other countries. Is travel wanderlust in the genes, too?

PART 3

LOOK ALIKES

Look Alikes

Sometimes the synchronicities, the messages that a particular adoption is especially right, come from the fact that two unrelated children born of different parents are adopted into one family and they look so much alike that everyone who sees them is convinced they are biological siblings.

Gradey and Daniel

When four-year old Daniel opened the door, I was confused. I thought he was Gradey, but he couldn't be Gradey; Gradey would be eight now! Right behind Daniel was his chuckling mom who quickly confirmed that my confusion was a common reaction.

Even Daniel's pre-kindergarten teacher, who also taught Gradey four years earlier, sometimes called Daniel by his older brother's name.

Their personalities are different, but they look like clones! These two boys with no genetic connection, look so much alike that their mom says she has to look at the back of their baby pictures to see whose name is written there and which of her boys is pictured.

Sydney and Simon

I opened the Sunday paper and noticed a story on the use of the Internet to connect potential birth and adoptive families.

There was a big photo of a child who looked familiar. It took me a moment to put a name to that face that sure looked like Sydney, a child whose placement I had been a part of a couple of years earlier. Then I read the caption beneath the picture. It wasn't Sydney, bur rather her brother Simon.

The similarities were amazing! I turned the page to continue reading the story and there was a picture showing the smiling faces of adoptive parents Craig and Kerry, with their son Simon. There were no pictures of Sydney in this article because it was about Craig and Kerry having met Simon's birth mother through the Internet.

Sydney and Simon both have round heads and blond hair. And Craig and Kerry keep in touch with both their kids' birth mothers through the Internet.

When Simon was welcomed into the family, Sydney's birth mother made a web page to announce the arrival of Simon, complete with editorial comments that told the story from the viewpoint of a proud birth mother!

Baby Brother Joins the Family

A couple of years after Veronica and Jack got their baby Sarah, I heard from an agency in Alabama that was looking for a home for a three-month-old baby boy whose ethnicity was believed to be a mixture of Caucasian and American Indian.

The baby had been in a foster home since birth while the agency checked with the Cherokee Tribe because the tribe could take custody if the child was determined to be Cherokee. He was finally free for adoption, because the tribe had responded that the alleged father was not an enrolled member of the tribe. If he had been, the Indian Child Welfare Act could have meant the tribe would take custody of the child and place him for adoption within the tribe.

In the months while the baby was in foster care, this little boy's complexion had darkened and he was beginning to look as if the he was part African-American. Now the agency needed a home for a baby boy who was said to be Cherokee but looked African-American.

The history of the Cherokee tribe is such that during the days of slavery, it was not uncommon for runaway slaves to be sheltered by and accepted into the Cherokee Tribe, and therefore not unusual for some Cherokees to have African-American blood lines and features. I've recently read that some Cherokees owned slaves!

When I heard of this child, I immediately thought of Jack and Veronica. I knew Veronica's ancestry included Cherokee, although she was not a registered tribal member, and the couple already had adopted a biracial child. They were ready for baby number two, and welcomed this little one into their home as quickly as Interstate Compact on Placement of Children in the sending and receiving states would issue approval.

Through the next few years, Veronica would send me photos of her two children, and we always marveled at how much this little girl and boy looked like blood siblings, even though (as far as we knew) they were not even the same ethnicity!

This will be one for DNA to solve!

Reassuring Grandma

We once had an adoptive mother who asked to meet with me as the pregnancy counselor to discuss the non-identifying information she'd been given by the adoption worker. Her mother-in-law, it seemed, had developed a fantasy that needed my intervention.

When Lily and Gerry, both African American, first talked to the adoption worker, they explained that their plan had always been to adopt two children and to have two biological children. They knew that African American children are often in foster care because there are fewer African American families who are willing to adopt.

In fact, I was working with an African American pregnancy client and we needed a family for her baby. Their little girl was about eighteen months old, and Lily was planning on weaning her from breast-feeding. Was this potential placement serious enough that she should keep her milk going for an adopted baby?

Their adoption worker explained that there's no guarantee about whether any mother will decide to relinquish her baby, but that we felt she was serious about her plan. And at any rate, she was due in a month, so Gerry and Lily wouldn't have to wait long to find out.

In trying to ascertain what might influence her decision, I asked Darnell, the African American pregnant client and single mother of three, if she had any relatives who might try to influence her decision, since it is not well accepted in her culture to consider adoption placement. "Oh, I've been through that before!" Darnell said, and told how her sister had promised to take her second child, rather than have the child placed outside the family. Her sister did take the boy – until her boyfriend left her and she lost her job -- and then Darnell's sister returned the child to her when he was three.

"I just don't have the same feeling as I do about my other children," Darnell said. I explained to her the theories of bonding and attachment, and helped her to understand that it might be the lack of time together as a newborn that caused problems between them. It made sense to her. She did feel that it was important for the adoptive couple to be with the child from as early as they could be.

Lily and Gerry did take placement as soon as the 72 hours were up and the papers were signed. Gerry was a full-bodied, dark skinned African-American; his wife was lighter skinned and their biological daughter was even fairer at two years than either of her parents. Everyone cooed as the baby boy was placed with them. He looked like his adoptive father!

In fact, he looked so much like the adoptive father that his own mother approached her daughter-in-law about a month after placement.

"She thinks I'm a saint!" Lily said. Everyone at church was exclaiming that the baby looked *just like* Gerry. His mother had developed a fantasy that *her son had fathered this child out-of-wedlock* and his saintly wife had accepted this child as her own!

Lily asked me to talk to her mother-in-law and assure her that this child was not Gerry's biological son!

So on the next adoption home visit, I accompanied the adoption worker and met the adoptive family and the grandmother and told her what the birth mother had said about the baby's father.

I described how they met, and that I had met him when he signed the adoption papers. I assured her the baby's father, just like the mother, sent his good wishes for his child to be raised in their family. Hopefully, she was convinced, and could help squelch the rumors going through their church community

.

Delayed Speech

It's not uncommon for parents who have adopted infants or small children to be worried when their child is delayed in his or her speech development. It's not an infrequent occurrence. At one time, I thought the pediatricians were looking for something to blame on adoption. I now believe, however, that the child is busy doing internal work, figuring out their life and maybe just needs some extra time to work it through. Recent research has identified this as adoption trauma.

I remember Trisha's little boy that she placed for adoption when he was two years old. Trisha was adopted herself as an infant and she knew very little about her background. Overshadowing whatever trauma she had as an adopted person, the searing trauma in her life occurred in the fourth grade when she came home from school to find all the relatives at her house, crying. "What's wrong?" she asked her favorite grandmother.

"Your mother had to go away," the grandmother replied. "She will be gone for a very long time." Another relative told her: "You won't see your mother again." Yet another relative told her, "Your mother is sleeping."

It was years before Trisha understood that her mother had died of cancer, after a short illness.

Knowing how children process information, I suspect that the grandmother's version might be different. She might think she told Trisha her mother died. Trisha remembers being told that her mother was gone. As a result, she tried for years to be good enough that her mother would return.

Children need to be told more than once, with information geared to their developmental level, when there is something difficult to understand. Something, one might say, as difficult to understand as death. Or adoption.

Trisha had confused the death of her mother and the fact that she was adopted. She didn't know what to believe. Raised as an only child, her father was loving but unapproachable when he came to discussing her adoption, saying that he didn't know anything about it; that it was his wife who arranged everything.

Trisha told me that, although her son Graham had been talking for six months, he had never called her *mama*. Trisha and Graham lived with her dad and they didn't see Graham's father; Graham never called anyone *dada*, either. First names were the only names he heard people call her, so he called her Trisha and her dad (his grandfather) was called Gary. "I think he's waiting until he has both a mommy and a daddy," said Trisha, who admitted she'd been thinking about adoption ever since she got pregnant. Now that Graham was getting older and Trisha had finished high school (much to the surprise of members of her own family who'd predicted that she'd drop out of school), she wanted to be a kid again. And she wanted to further her education so she'd be able to make more money than working retail.

When I first met Trisha and saw Graham, I was struck by how much they looked like one of the families waiting for a child with our agency! Trisha looked like she could be a relative of theirs. After placement, they even joked together about where their relatives had been when Trisha had been conceived!

Graham was one of those kids whose pediatrician said he was speech delayed. They had his hearing tested and they took him for speech therapy. About two months later, the new mom was saying, "Yep, he started talking and now he won't quit!" In the background, I could hear him chattering away contentedly.

Meanwhile, Trisha was working through her own issues about adoption. She asked to attend the adoption hearing of her own son; she wanted to know just how 'adoption happened.'

Trisha was the only birth parent I've had who was at the adoption hearing of her child; I believe she was working on her own adoption issues, then. The last time I saw her, she was still trying to locate her birth mother.

PART 4

STRANGE BUT TRUE
STORIES OF
BIRTH AND ADOPTION

Strange But True Stories of Birth and Adoption

Some of the stories in this section are about secret pregnancies. I've been fascinated by this facet of adoption for years. How is it possible for a woman to hide a pregnancy for nine months? Impossible, say some folks who have watched bulging bellies firsthand. Not impossible, I say, having witnessed many of them through the years.

Sometimes the secret pregnancies are merely secret from "other people" (the ones that my mother always worried about, as in "what will *other people* think?").

Sometimes the secret pregnancies are known only in the heart of the mother. And sometimes the denial is so strong that even the mother doesn't know about it until the birth!

Some of these stories are about what we call "drop-in babies," babies that we don't know about until we get a call from the birth mother or the hospital staff after a baby is born. Sometimes these are women who have dealt with their pregnancies by ignoring them, pretending they aren't pregnant, and hoping they won't be.

They don't seek prenatal care and it may be because they don't know they will qualify for medical care from the state.

Sometimes (but less often than the general public might think) these women are involved in the drug scene, as you will see in some of these stories. After observing this phenomenon for many years, I believe that the reason for many secret pregnancies without prenatal care is the lack of emotional support for birth mothers planning an adoption in our culture. It's not the pregnancy she wants to hide, but the adoption. She fears condemnation for making this life-giving decision.

The Bathtub Baby

It was wintertime when Caileigh was born. Her fourteen-year-old birth mom Elaine had successfully hidden her pregnancy from everyone by wearing baggy jeans and flannel shirts over loose T-shirts.

Elaine's mother had left the family when Elaine was six years old and her little sister was four. Her dad worked hard in construction to keep a roof over their heads and to provide for his family. Because construction workers start their jobs early, their father was usually out of the house by 4:30 A.M.

On this particular morning, Elaine was lying in bed waiting to hear her dad's truck pull out of the driveway. Her back hurt. Sometimes when her back hurt like that, she could make it stop by taking a warm bath. As soon as she was certain he'd left, she quietly got out of bed.

She didn't want to awaken her friend sleeping in her sister's bed. Her sister was spending the night with a friend, so Polly had come over to spend the night with Elaine.

Elaine filled the tub and eased herself into the water. It wasn't long before she felt like she needed to go to the bathroom. She glanced down at herself and was horrified to see two little feet coming out of her body! She stepped back into the tub as her body convulsed in an involuntary push and suddenly there was this perfect, tiny baby girl in the bath water with her. Eventually, Elaine struggled to her feet, holding the baby, to turn the shower on and clean up herself and the baby. As she reached to adjust the showerhead, a big "something" fell out of her body.

"At first I thought it was my stomach," Elaine told me. "But then I remembered 'afterbirth' and I decided that's what it was." She calmly tied off the umbilicus, gathered a plastic bag, and placed the placenta in it.

Then she got out her sister's doll blanket, took the paper diaper and toy bottle from a doll, put whole milk in the bottle, and went back to bed with the baby. When her friend awoke a while later, Elaine greeted her with, "Look what I did!"

Polly shrieked. "What will we do?" she asked. A panicked call to Polly's mother brought help and a quick trip to the closest emergency room, and the hospital social worker called me.

When I met Elaine, I asked her how she had known what to do and she told me she'd watched a dog have puppies. She quickly added that she had also asked a lot of questions in sex education class. The other kids had snickered and laughed at her when she asked questions. "But how else was I gonna find out? I didn't have anybody to talk to!"

In shock and unprepared for parenthood, Elaine and her family thought it best to put the baby into a receiving home while they worked out a plan.

We found the birth father, a fifteen-year-old, good-looking, street-wise kid named Eddy who was staying with different friends a week at a time. He agreed to come to the office and fill out the background papers. His family got involved and one of his uncles seriously proposed to take the baby and give it to his childless sister as a birthday surprise. After all, he reasoned, she'd always wanted a baby and didn't have one!

Elaine and Eddy continued to consider other possible families and decided they'd like to meet one of our waiting couples, Rebecca and Guil and their son. They visited the prospective couple in their home one Sunday and Elaine decided they could be the baby's forever family.

On the day Elaine and Eddy were scheduled to sign adoption papers, however, Eddy was a "no show" and she decided she wanted to think about it a bit longer.

Caileigh was growing stronger. Starting at five pounds, six ounces, she was quickly gaining weight in the receiving home. Eddy and Elaine both came to visit the baby. They couldn't decide what they should do. Finally, since she didn't feel ready to give up on parenting, Elaine's dad relaxed a bit in his stand and said she could take the baby home.

Six weeks later, I came back from vacation to learn that Elaine had called and asked if Guil and Rebecca were still interested in taking the baby. Elaine had tried being a parent.

All her good buddies — kids from twelve to sixteen years of age who'd said they would help (one had even offered to shoplift formula if she needed him to!) — were off following their own teenage interests and Elaine was feeling like she really ought to be back in school. The special counselor from the child welfare department who had been helping her set goals and work out an education plan was supportive of Elaine's plan for adoption.

Rebecca and Guil were overjoyed to open their hearts and their home to Elaine's baby. They sent pictures for years, and Elaine graduated from high school in the spring. Rebecca asked her at Christmas, "What made you decide to get it together and go back to school?"

"Giving Caileigh to you," Elaine answered. "I knew I couldn't let my life waste away I had made a great sacrifice so she could have a better life. I want her to be proud of me someday."

Today, Elaine and Rebecca (and Caileigh) have contact through FaceBook. Caileigh is about to graduate from high school, and Elaine has children she is raising, including a new little baby girl.

One More for the Road

The caller identified himself simply as Joe. He said that he and his girlfriend Laura were at the hospital where she'd just given birth to a baby boy and they wanted to place him for adoption. I told him I would be there as soon as I could but that first I needed to know what kind of a family they wanted for the baby. He said, "Someone to give him lots of love." Then he added, "We've done this before."

The phone was in the cradle before I put the names together with the events of nineteen months ago. I recalled that November afternoon when a truck driver named Joe had appeared at the Flagstaff Regional Medical Center just off Interstate 40 with a girlfriend named Laura whose water broke as they drove through Arizona. I wasn't directly involved in that case, but I remembered many of the details — a tall, blonde birth mother, a baby girl who weighed almost ten pounds, and a birth father who was in a hurry to leave town because he had a load to deliver and was unhappy about having to wait the required three days before papers could be signed.

It was the same couple. This time, they were trying to get to California before the baby was born because there, they had learned, the papers could be signed right after delivery. Their plan to get to California didn't work out. Once again, Laura's water broke while they were in Arizona (this time, near Phoenix) and they were lucky to get to the hospital just in time for little Casey to be born. Joe stayed for the baby's arrival but left before I got there, to take his cargo to Los Angeles. Laura said he planned to return to Arizona in time to pick up a load of cantaloupe from the fields outside of Yuma to truck back to Memphis. He wanted the adoption papers ready to sign at that time so they could be on the road again.

The adoptive parents of two years ago were delighted to hear there was a second baby, a full sibling to the first, who could become theirs, too. They happily drove to the hospital for a visit again with the birth mother of their daughter. They were indeed ready for another child. The birth mother told me when she signed the papers three days later, "I feel like I'm leaving the babies with family. This was meant to be."

A Turnaround Trip

When I worked for Southwest Adoption Center, I traveled back and forth for weekly meetings from my home office in Tucson to the Scottsdale headquarters, a good two-hour trip by car. One of the experiments the agency tried was to have me take a plane to see if that would save time. It didn't work very well because by the time I drove to the airport in Tucson, found a parking place, flew the forty-five-minute ride to Phoenix, was met by someone from the office, and then driven to Scottsdale, it still took two hours!

What the agency was paying me for gas mileage was less than the price of the plane ticket. Still, we tried it a few times to see which was more effective.

On my arrival in the Phoenix airport one morning, the driver from the office met me as I got off the plane and said, "You have to turn around and go back. We had a call after you left from a birth mother in Tucson who gave birth last night, at home. She wants to meet with someone immediately." So I purchased a return ticket and caught the next plane back to Tucson.

Finding Sarah wasn't difficult. She lived at an apartment near one of Tucson's biggest hospitals. Thirty years old, Sarah worked for a veterinarian and often took abandoned or sick animals home with her so she could personally give them the tender loving care they needed. She had hidden her pregnancy well under the smocks she was required to wear at work. No one suspected anything when she packed up some surgical tools and took them home with her one day. She delivered her baby girl all by herself in her apartment.

When I arrived, I began taking down her information about the delivery. I asked her what time had the baby had been born the previous evening. "It was before *Moonlighting* started, so it was over before seven o'clock. I wanted to have everything cleaned up so I could watch Bruce Willis. It's my favorite TV show."

With Sarah's permission, I took her baby to the nearby hospital to be checked over and to have the birth registered. The baby girl (I called her Cybil, of course!) went to a receiving home while we worked out the details of a placement. Sarah opted not to meet the family she chose — they loved animals — who arrived two days later.

When the adoptive father read through the background forms at placement, he looked up in amazement. "Your office is good! You told us you do matching, but I didn't know it would be this close! We're German and Polish, just like the birth mother. And now this! It says she had an operation for strabismus when she was little. Well, so did I!"

I didn't tell him it was just a coincidence and that we hadn't even known about his crossed-eye operation as a child! Secretly, however, I knew then that the match was controlled by a higher office than our personnel in Scottsdale!

Almost a Dumpster Baby

We got a call from a hospital the day after Martin Luther King holiday. An undocumented worker from Mexico had appeared at the hospital with a baby girl wrapped in a towel. The twenty-three-year old mom, who spoke only Spanish, gave her name as Maria. She had the baby at home, but couldn't get the placenta out, so she had wrapped the baby in a towel and called a cab to take her to the nearest hospital.

Maria said she had been threatened (it was unclear by whom) that if she messed up, she'd be sent back to Mexico. Fearful of being deported, she had told no one about her pregnancy. The nurse who interpreted for her said that if she'd been able to get the placenta out, Maria would not have come to the hospital. We're not sure what would have happened to the baby, but it's not inconceivable she might have been found abandoned somewhere. The hospital's doctors declared that Maria could go home, but the baby needed to stay in the hospital another day for observation.

The day we met, Maria chose from the prospective adoptive couples' profiles a particular Hispanic family, one without any kids. Maria said if she decided to keep the baby, she would return to the hospital the next day and take her home. She didn't, so late Wednesday afternoon I put the baby into temporary care.

Maria had my business card and she had the numbers of two nurses at the hospital that spoke Spanish. She didn't call any of us. The hospital billing office called to tell me the address she had given had been a false address and to ask if she'd given a different address to the agency. At the phone number she had given, no one claimed to know her.

By Friday, the adoptive couple who had been chosen by Maria and who had been notified by their worker, was calling me and begging to take the baby home. They reasoned if this were an abandoned baby, we'd have to wait three to six months to terminate the parental rights in court; they'd rather have the baby with them than in a foster home. If the mother came in and wanted her baby back, they knew they could return the child to her. They would take the risk.

Then they told me how they knew the baby was meant for them. They were told the birth mother had named the baby Christina. They had planned since before they married that their first daughter would be named Kristina, after the friend who had introduced them.

On Sunday, a Spanish-speaking coworker and I scoured the neighborhood near the fake address, looking for Maria, leaving messages with several people. Maria called early the next morning and set an appointment for two days later. She asked to meet the adoptive parents and to see her baby again. She wasn't sure, but she thought she probably would sign the papers to allow them to adopt the baby.

Although Melissa is Hispanic and had grown up speaking Spanish, she didn't feel confident enough to do this alone, so they brought a friend to help them speak to Maria in Spanish. When Maria asked to have time alone with the baby, John and Melissa and their friend waited in my office while Maria (in another room) held the baby for a long time, rocking her, and singing to her in a soft voice. We left her alone to think her thoughts.

The co-worker who had helped me look for Maria came in, and we checked on her every few minutes to see if Maria wanted to talk. For a long time, she did not. She just held the baby and rocked her. Finally, the Spanish-speaking counselor went in alone and spoke with her. Melissa and John and I sat together in my office.

"I will die if she doesn't say we can keep her," cried Melissa. We spoke of the special bond that had developed so much more quickly than they had imagined it could, and how in just three short days, Kristina had taken a big part of their hearts.

Finally the worker emerged from the office and said Maria had decided to sign the papers and let John and Melissa take her home. We all went into the office and Melissa and John tearfully told Maria what a gift they considered this baby to be.

In a spontaneous gesture, Melissa stood and removed the necklace from around her neck. She said, with her friend translating into Spanish, "John gave me this necklace. It is my favorite piece of jewelry and I wear it all the time. I want you to have it. You can keep it next to your heart, and know that we will always hold you in our hearts."

She asked Maria's permission to place the necklace around Maria's neck. Maria agreed. As Melissa fixed the clasp, John said (and their friend translated), "Every time you look in the mirror and see this necklace, know that we love you."

Six weeks later, Maria called out of the blue and asked if she could visit them again. This time I picked her up and drove her to the East Valley office of Catholic Social Service, which was nearer John and Melissa's house. Maria was wearing the necklace. We all visited, and Melissa had boned up on her Spanish enough that she talked directly to Maria this time. But just in case, she had brought her mother who speaks Spanish fluently. Maria was peaceful when I drove her home that evening after a lengthy visit. John and Melissa have since been very helpful in talking to other parents who are waiting for placement.

Agua

I have noticed through the years that placement varieties come in "clumps." We might not have a need for foster care (or receiving home care, as we now call it) for a long time, then we'll have five babies in a row who need it. And one year, we had nine Indian Child Welfare Act cases in a short period of time.

At the time of this story, we were on a run of Spanish-only speakers. These are always a challenge for us. We utilize volunteers and seek to hire bilingual staff whenever we have openings, but it's difficult to retain them as employees. A well-trained bilingual worker can always find a job making more money than in the non-profit field.

Thankfully, the bilingual staff at other programs of Catholic Social Service has been very willing to help us with translating. Our Phoenix office of Catholic Social Service has an award-winning refugee and immigration department, and there are over twenty different languages spoken in our office. We've even called on them to decipher Chinese characters in a note left with a baby girl who was adopted from China!

When possible, we try to match our Spanish-only birth moms with an adoptive parent who speaks Spanish, so that one chosen parent will be able to inform the birth mother directly of the love they feel for her and for her baby. This is very comforting for the birth mothers, and she deserves to know how much the baby is loved.

A few pregnant women have been referred to us by another agency prior to the delivery, in which case we have a little time to get acquainted. Often these are women who not only can't speak English, but also have a background of extreme poverty and lack of education, not as a result of a lack of intelligence, but rather a lack of opportunity. One of these young women was Rosario.

Rosario needed prenatal care but did not qualify due to her status as an undocumented worker. She had no transportation and did not speak English. We referred her to an obstetrician who was fluent in Spanish, which was a great relief to her. The agency would pay for her prenatal care, and the delivery would be covered under the Federal Emergency Medical Assistance act.

I thought that Rosario understood our signal, which was for her to page me and say "hospital," if she went into labor; I would know it was time for me to drive her to the hospital. At two-thirty on a Saturday morning two weeks before her expected due date, I got a call, but I could only hear heavy breathing. I figured it had to be Rosario, so I called her back.

When she answered, all she could say was, *"mucho dolor!"* which I understood: "much pain." I assured her I would be there *andale*. Her roommate was ready to keep her little boy while we got to the hospital as fast we legally could. About three miles away from the hospital, she said, *"agua!"* I was pretty sure she wasn't thirsty.

At the emergency room entrance, I ran in and said I had a woman in hard labor in my car and she could only speak Spanish.

Luckily, the desk clerk on duty was Hispanic, and she came with the wheelchair personnel to whisk Rosario away. "Did her water break?" she asked. "Oh, yes, I see that it did."

I moved the car out of the emergency room driveway. About a minute later I was back inside the hospital and asking where they had taken Rosario. "Room three," the attendant answered, "but her baby's already here!"

I walked into the room and found a nurse standing by the baby in a warmer, and four nurses pushing towels with their feet, mopping the floor. Rosario was lying on the bed, still in her clothes. "How did she deliver?" I asked in astonishment. "She still has on her clothes!"

"*Through* the clothes," said the nurse. She explained that when they stood her to move her from the wheelchair to the bed, the baby fell out of her! That amniotic fluid is slippery stuff!

Later in the day, the adoptive parents came to the hospital to meet Rosario. At first reluctant to meet, I knew that the adoptive mom's ability to speak Spanish would reassure Rosario in ways I could not. We took pictures of them together, so that someday J-J (the nickname they gave the baby) would know what his birth mother looks like.

A few months later, Rosario asked for a letter from the adoptive mom, which she supplied in Spanish, but at present Rosario does not want to have any photos. We will honor her wishes, but the photos will remain in the file in case Rosario asks for them.

The Journey

I remember a little girl I placed through Southwest Adoption Center in the late 1980s. She was almost two years old at the time. Her birth mom and dad had wanted a better life for her. The birth mother said that her own mother had gone crazy and then abandoned her when she was the same age of her daughter. This young mother was now having serious misgivings about her own ability to parent since she had not been adequately parented herself beyond that age. I recommended we find counseling or parenting education for her, but she was insistent that the baby be placed for adoption, as she wished her mother had done for her.

The family chosen for this little girl lived in another state. That particular state required that the adoption papers be signed in our state before that state would allow the adoptive parents to travel to our state. The adoption agency's director wanted me to take the consents, call the adoptive couple to let them know it was safe to travel, then spend the night with the baby at a motel while the family flew to Arizona. The prospect of spending the night with a frightened two-year-old to whom I was a stranger was not at all appealing. The birth parents offered their couch and suggested that I stay with them so they could all be together one last night. Certainly this was unconventional social work practice, but I agreed, believing it to be in the child's best interest. I was somewhat dismayed that this young couple did not, at least in my presence, discuss with the little girl what was happening.

In the car the next morning as I was driving the twenty-five miles or so to where the new family was waiting, the little girl sat in the front seat with me. (This was before booster seats were required, and certainly before children were placed in the back seat for safety's sake.)

As I drove, I explained to this little one that her mommy and daddy loved her so very much and that they no longer could take care of her. Her gaze was so intent that I felt she was looking at me with "soul eyes." I told her I was taking her to meet her new mommy and daddy and that they would give her lots of love.

I told her, however, that she was to remember that her first mommy and daddy also loved her very much. She said not a word, nor did she indicate she heard me. When I finished my short speech, she peacefully closed her eyes and leaned back, and napped the rest of the way.

I turned up the volume on the radio. The sound of Grand Funk Railroad's *I'm Your Captain* lent an ironic eeriness to the occasion: "I'm getting closer to my ho-ome. I'm getting closer to my ho-ome."

Dawn

Dawn was a birth mom who looked forward to new pictures of her baby she'd placed for adoption. But the more she looked at them as the child grew older, the less certain she was about who the father might be. She had named Brian as the birth father. Brian indicated in no uncertain terms that he didn't want the burden of supporting a child and readily signed the adoption consents. Her uncertainty about the baby's father was beginning to gnaw away at her. In her pride, Dawn had shown the pictures to the mother of Tad, an old boyfriend whom she'd been seeing just before the weekend that she was so sure had produced the pregnancy. Tad's mother remarked upon seeing the photographs of the six-month-old baby, "She looks just like my son!" This bothered Dawn. What if Tad or his mother decided he was the baby's father? Could he be? Dawn called me and shared her concerns. (This was before DNA testing was available to clarify the issue.)

Understandably, had the adoptive parents known of her call, their fear might have been that Dawn was hoping that Tad was actually the birth father and that he might help her get the baby back. But that wasn't Dawn's intention. She was worried that Tad's mother might intervene.

With my encouragement, Dawn approached Tad and talked to him about it. He agreed that he wasn't ready to take on the care of a child and he surely didn't want his mother trying to make him feel guilty for anything he might have done.

He also agreed to sign adoption papers, just in case he was the birth father. The papers were filed with the court and Dawn felt at peace again. Her baby would be safe in her new home.

PART 5

ALL GROWN UP
Adult Adoptee Stories

Adult Adoptee Stories

In 1979, the first year I worked in adoptions, we had a total of three contacts (that I knew of) that involved researching an old file. By the time I left eight years later, we were having more than thirty such contacts in a year.

By state law, Arizona adoption agencies are required to keep adoption records for 99 years. Arizona Children's Home Association had been formed as an orphanage in 1912 and incorporated in 1914, which as Arizona history goes, is a long time ago.

I once was asked to research case number 003. We found it in a crumbling file folder along with scant information on the first ten or so residents of Arizona Children's Home. The third generation beyond that child was doing genealogical research and hoped to find out his ancestors' parents' names prior to his being adopted into the family whose name they all bore. There was very little information in the file, just the mother's first and last name. The father's first name did not appear.

Some of those contacts that required research would be requests for non-identifying information (which until the law changed in the 1990s was all we could give) for adoptees who desperately needed answers to their health related questions. Some were updates of information that would start out with something like: *My name used to be Jane Smith, and in 1968, I placed a child for adoption. If my child ever wants to find me, my current name is Jane Swartz and my sister Betty Smith will always know how to reach me.*

Many of those women from long ago were not sure of the date of the birth of the child. Some women were in therapy and asked for copies of the case notes from their file because they were having trouble making sense out of their past. Some contacts were from adoptive parents with teenagers, and the parents were hoping to find something in the birth parents' background to explain the child's current behavior on.

Here are some stories where the element of "more than chance" came to light many years after placement.

My First Reunion

The first adoption meeting between adult adoptee and birth parent that I took part in was in the mid-1980s at the Arizona Children's Home Association (now called Arizona's Children Association). During the 1950-60s, during the days of shame and secrecy, ACHA did a lot of adoptions, about a hundred a year. "Send Susie to Arizona to stay with a sick aunt" and then Susie was supposed to go back home to Pennsylvania and pretend she hadn't had a baby.

We would occasionally get letters in the mail from birth mothers of that era whose children placed for adoption were about to become adults. With that significant event, these birth parents thought (or hoped) a search would begin. Many birth parents express that they feel unworthy to do a search, but quickly add that if the child wants to find the parent, they would be glad to meet them.

Such was the letter I received one March from Daphne. She gave her birth daughter's date of birth, her own current last name and address, and a notarized statement giving permission to give her name to her birth daughter. I put her letter in with some others to be sent to the off-site location where we kept old files and didn't think anymore about it.

A few weeks later, I got a call from Sonya, an adoptive mother whose daughter Tara had just turned eighteen. Sonya wanted to know how to get a copy of her daughter's original birth certificate with the birth parents' names. At the time Sonya and her husband adopted Tara, they had been told that their daughter could have this information when she reached the age of majority. She was dismayed to hear that the law had changed retroactively, closing all adoption records.

"This makes me a liar!" she complained vehemently. "My daughter has asked about her birth mother since she was eight years old and I've always told her that when she turned eighteen, we'll look for her birth mother."

Our instructions at that time were to give, when asked, only non-identifying information from the file to either side of the adoption. We did not, however, do active searches. I told Sonya that I would pull the file from storage and send her whatever information I could. When I checked the cross-reference cards, I suddenly realized that I had already requested the file so I could place Daphne's letter in it. I held a match in my hands!

I approached the agency director for advice on what to do. Since we were dealing with adults, he suggested having the adoptive parents and the adoptee write a letter saying they were requesting to have identifying information released and then get in touch with both sides and introduce them.

First, I called Tara's mom and told her that I had a letter in the file for Tara and suggested Tara meet with me to prepare her for contact with her birth mother. Tara was to bring in a letter from her parents giving permission for contact.

On Friday morning, Tara brought the letter to my office. She was a tall girl, five feet eleven inches, with blonde, shoulder-length hair that she wore with bangs and a grown-out permanent with waves starting about temple level. Tara wore a red sundress with spaghetti straps and with a ruffle on the bottom. She told me she had wanted to meet her birth mother since she was eight. This need intensified during the last year when she had spent time volunteering with abused children. She said this developed within her an overpowering desire to thank her birth mother for giving her a positive life experience with her adoptive parents.

That afternoon, Daphne came to the office for her "prepare-to-meet" interview. To my astonishment, Daphne wore her shoulder-length brown hair in the same style as Tara's, complete with a grown-out permanent, bangs and a middle part. And even harder to believe, Daphne had on a sundress strikingly similar to the one Tara was wearing that morning, only hers was of blue and white stripes. I was absolutely amazed at the similarities.

Daphne called Tara from my office and they decided to meet at a park. "How will I know you?" asked Tara.

"Beth says our hair is fixed the same way," Daphne answered. "And she says we're wearing the same dress except a different color!"

Sonya, the adoptive mother, later told me that ever since her daughter mentioned that she wanted to find her birth mother, she'd imagined they would search to the ends of the earth and finally, perhaps after two or three years, find her. She was a bit overcome with the suddenness of the find! When she met Daphne, however, she said they spontaneously embraced, and in that hug, although much smaller in stature than Tara, Daphne's bones felt the same as her daughter's.

Finding her birth mother helped Tara to feel more complete, and Sonya and her husband welcomed Daphne into their lives like a long lost relative.

The Note in the File

I'd received news over the weekend that my dad had died and I was in the office Monday getting some things together so I could leave for the funeral. I didn't have time for an unscheduled visit from an outsider.

I heard an official-sounding voice in the lobby asking for me. I peeked around the corner and my instinct told me that it was a police officer. He looked as though he was there to serve papers. What could this possibly be about?

I was partially right. Richard was indeed a Phoenix policeman who was in Tucson for the day. He had been doing some investigating on his own, he said rather brusquely, and had learned he was adopted twenty-eight years ago through our agency.

He told me his mom had died a few years earlier and now he wanted to find his "other mother," the one who had placed him for adoption. When I explained my personal predicament, the "cop" personae left and Richard turned into a warm human being. I told him I would put in the request for his file and when I got back from Texas I would research his case and write to him.

When I returned to work and had time to look at Richard's file, I found a very interesting case. Richard's birth mother had been twenty-eight years old at the time (the same age he was now), single and pregnant.

She was blinded by diabetes and felt she couldn't raise a child by herself, especially on the salary she earned as a church secretary. Because her sight had begun to leave her after she was grown, she'd taught herself to do many things, including to touch-type.

In the file, there was a half-sheet of paper upon which Doris had typed a note to her social worker. Doris wrote that although it was not the usual thing, the nurse at the hospital had let her hold her baby so she could examine him and know that he was okay. She had told the baby that God was going to give him a home where he would be loved, and she wanted him to know that God would take care of him. The note was signed, simply, "Doris."

I also had Richard's adoption file. I knew that his adoptive mother was also named Doris. Neither he nor his adoptive parents had known that this was also his birth mother's name. I made a copy of the note and put the copy in the file. I mailed the original to Richard at his home in Phoenix, along with the non-identifying information about his birth mother.

He called me as soon as he got my letter. Knowing that she was blind made all the difference in the world to him. He had been afraid it was something wrong with *him* that caused him to be placed for adoption. He wanted to find her and let her know he'd come out all right.

Richard's detective work paid off. It didn't take him long to find the blind woman who had worked as a church secretary during her pregnancy. He brought her to my office to meet me.

Doris was overwhelmed. Living childless for all of her fifty-six years, she expressed delight to suddenly discover that she was a grandma!

A Change of Faith

How does an adoption agency always have "just the right family" for every baby? The answer, of course, is they don't. In my experience, it's very important that agencies that share the same values also share their family resources.

That way, when an agency doesn't have the right match between adoptive child and adoptive family, the staff can network with other agencies in the area. Better to go outside the agency and make a good "shared placement" than make a poor match! When I worked at Arizona Children's Home Association in Tucson, one of the agencies with whom we frequently networked was Catholic Social Service in Tucson.

Many years ago, I had a call about a previously networked case between Catholic Social Service and Arizona Children's Home Association in Tucson. The Catholic Social Service worker called to say she'd been working with a woman who had placed a child with them twelve years earlier. Her only request they couldn't meet at the time was to place the baby with a Catholic family.

(Many people assume that a religious-based agency works only with families of the same faith, that usually is not so, although it may be true with some agencies.) At that particular time, Catholic Social Service in Tucson had called on ACHA for a Catholic family for this baby girl.

Now, twelve years later, the birth mother's father had been diagnosed with a devastating neurological disease that is hereditary.

The birth mother had done a lot of research and came to meet me to tell me the severity of the issue.

If caught early enough, there is help for the person who has it. I agreed to interview her and evaluate the situation. The birth mother, now married with children of her own, felt it was imperative that the family who had adopted her first child be given the information about the disease. She had collected brochures about the disease and information about a local support group. I told her I would contact the family and have them come in to share information.

(This was long enough ago that there was no thought of having her deliver the information in person. It simply wasn't done in those days.)

I asked her if there was anything else she wanted me to tell them when I met with them. She looked down at her hands in her lap and said seriously, "Yes, there is. I know they received my daughter because I asked for a Catholic family for her." She looked up; I could see the concern etched on her face. "But I'm not Catholic any more. Five years ago, I joined the Baptist Church. Now I'm worried that she might be with a family who is too strictly Catholic." I promised to ask, and to call her after I met with the family.

I invited the adoptive family to come to my office, telling them I had something of extreme importance to share with them about health issues for their daughter. Their first fear was that the birth mother wanted to take back the child they had loved for twelve years. I assured them that it was a health-related issue, not a custody-related issue. They agreed to come in the next day.

After giving them the medical information, which was the purpose of the visit, they began to inquire about the birth mother and her family. I told them this woman had children of her own who were half-siblings of their daughter and that they all knew about this child who had been placed outside the family. They gave me some updated information about their daughter to share, including the kind of activities she participated in and some stories of their special connection to tell her birth mother.

I told them I would be talking with the birth mother again and asked if there was anything they wanted me to pass along to her. The wife said, "We are afraid to mention it because we know we have our daughter because we were Catholic, but we aren't Catholic any more! A few years ago we joined the Baptist Church and my husband is now an ordained minister."

Of course, they didn't understand my spontaneous laughter until I told them the birth mother's religious transformation. "God works in wondrous ways," said the adoptive father and minister.

The Chosen Baby

Adoption agencies provide many important services that aren't immediately apparent to the outside world. One is providing information for people who were adopted through the agency. In the days before adoption searches were accepted practice and legal, we could only give non-identifying information (*i.e.,* everything but last names and addresses) to those with an immediate link to the placement: birth parent, adoptive parent, or adult adoptee.

Prior to the 1980s, information given to a parent at the time of placement was often given verbally, not written down, and was edited to fit an image of expectation rather than the truth. After all, that was a time when "experts knew what was best" for others.

Social workers from that era admit that the best minds involved in adoptions then believed fully in the power of environment and thought that if adoptive parents were told nothing about the child's background, the child had a better chance of becoming like the adoptive parents.

Known as the *tabula rasa* theory of child development, the child was believed to be a "blank slate" upon which the new parents could write their beliefs, values, and characteristics.

It was in that era that a book titled *The Chosen Baby* was written. *The Chosen Baby* was one of the first children's books written to explain adoption to the adopted child. In simple language and with wispy drawings, the story is told of Mr. and Mrs. Brown who had everything they wanted in life except a tiny baby of their own to love. Mr. and Mrs. Brown go to see nice Mrs. White at the adoption agency and after she asks them a lot of questions, she takes them into a room where there are rows and rows of little babies in little cribs. Mr. and Mrs. Brown look at all the babies until they find "just the right one" which they choose for their very own.

Although I've known many people raised on this story who take special pride in being chosen, critics say that once children can reason that if they could be "chosen," then they could be "unchosen," and will worry about being sent back. But that's not the interpretation that Mary of Phoenix told me about.

A few years into my adoptions career, I was asked to do a non-identifying information write-up for Mary, a woman in her thirties who called the Tucson ACHA office and asked for any information about her background.

Mary lived in Phoenix where she was married, had a family of her own, and where she worked as a teacher. Mary said she'd had always been curious about her background and now that she had children, she would like to have medical information to answer their pediatrician's questions. I promised to pull the file, read through it, and give her any medical information I found.

Unlike the majority of cases from the 1950s, I learned upon reading her file that Mary's birth parents were married instead of single. Mary's birth father had suffered a nervous breakdown while in the military and had been hospitalized.

His wife had been emotionally supportive of her husband who had received a medical discharge from the military. He had been hospitalized as a civilian at the time Mary's birth mother learned she was pregnant. Her husband needed her undivided attention, and so they made a plan to place Mary for adoption.

I would have preferred to give her this information in person, but as a young working mother with responsibilities, she couldn't take off time to come to Tucson. She sounded stable enough to handle this in writing, and I wrote up her background information as sensitively as I could and mailed it to her.

Mary wrote back a very kind letter. She was surprised to learn her parents were married, but not alarmed by her birth father's mental illness. Her adoptive mother had been in and out of mental hospitals all her life, Mary said, and she knew the difficulties her family had had in staying together. More than anything, she realized from the information I'd given her that she had not been defective and thus rejected. Her adoption didn't have anything to do with any fault of hers when she was small. It had everything to do, however, with her birth parents' situation.

"My parents had this book, *The Chosen Child*, which they would read to me. I know they wanted me to feel good. My dad enlarged upon the story by telling me they went to this old deserted grocery store in Tucson where there were rows and rows of babies and they picked out their favorite one. He meant to make me feel good about being chosen, but all I could relate to was going to the pound to choose a puppy. I was always drawn to the most pitiful puppy, the one that looked lonely and scrawny, the runt of the litter.

I always thought I must have been the most pitiful one there and that's why they took me!"

For my part, I was amazed at the fallibility of the adoption agency. Here was a child whose birth parents made an adoption plan because of mental illness that would keep them from attending fully to the needs of the child and the agency had placed her with a family that had the same problem!

I pulled the adoption file and pored over it. Were there indications in the file of problems lurking in the future for the adoptive mother's mental health? No, there were not. Instead, there were glowing statements of reference from family and friends. There was no indication whatsoever of any problems in the medical statement from the doctor. Finally, I marveled at the serendipity of placement. Was this child destined to live with mental illness no matter the plan of her original family?

Muscle Men

One of my favorite stories about searches is one I've told and retold through the years. It's about Steve, a man who called me when he was twenty-seven years old. He told me his adoptive mother had died a couple of years earlier and he thought about his birth mother especially on Mother's Day. He'd decided he would look for her.

I explained that I could only give him non-identifying information, but that I knew lots of people who had taken that and pieced together enough information to do their own successful search.

We had a group of adoptees and birth parents in Tucson who taught each other how to search. They called their organization Triad, an acronym standing for Truth Resulting In Adoption Discoveries. I told him that after I did some research, he could take the non-identifying information to the meetings and see if they could help him find his birth family. I would pull his file and call him for an interview when I had something for him.

I had fun reading this old file that told of a sixteen-year-old high school girl who played clarinet in the marching band. She'd fallen in love with a high school senior who played trombone in the marching band as well as in a jazz combo. He was handsome and muscled. He'd lifted weights and played baseball, football, and track. He entered and won the Mr. Arizona contest (a muscle-building show) his high school senior year.

On the day Steve came to the office to read his typewritten background, I went to the lobby to greet him. It was summertime and here was a good looking, deeply tanned young man, dressed in a "muscle shirt" that showed off his very broad shoulders! He came into my office and sat quietly reading what I'd written.

When he finished, he looked up, and grinned. "I came in thinking I wanted to meet my birth mother. Now I feel I have to meet my birth father. He sounds just like me!" He told me that he had played the same sports in school, that he played jazz guitar in a combo, and he lifted weights and won the Mr. Arizona contest!

I was flabbergasted. "Did you know any of this? Were you placed in an athletic family?" I asked, "At least, one that encouraged you in sports?"

"No, they were all bookworms. They would all be back at the house with their noses stuck in books and I was at the park playing a pick-up game of baseball or football."

Several years later I saw one of the people who had been involved with Triad. I mentioned that I had always wondered if Steven found his birth parents. She told me that he had and that they had developed a good relationship

Are You The Same Beth?

I was standing in the checkout line at the grocery store where I often shopped, when the young female clerk read my name on my check and asked if I was the same person who worked at Arizona Children's Home. I said that I was.

"I've called and talked to you before, about doing a search for my birth parents," she said. "I was adopted from Arizona Children's Home. I'm Stacy," and then she gave me her last name.

I remembered her because she'd gone to school with my stepdaughter who was also named Stacy. She had never come in to get the background information I'd written up. I wondered if I'd scared her away.

"I've gotten married and had my first baby, and I've just been too busy to call you back." I invited her to call for an appointment. I still had her background in my office.

A few weeks later, Stacy came in and learned that her birth mother's first name was Margie and that she came from a state in the Midwest that had a large river in it. Her birth mother had been sent to Tucson "to help a sick aunt." She attended high school in Tucson and then returned to her hometown. She played flute, liked to draw, and was healthy. That was about all there was. Stacy was off to Triad to begin her search. Many months later I learned how her search had ended.

Triad, like many search organizations, keeps lots of high school yearbooks. The year of her birth, Stacy learned, there were only three high schools in Tucson. She looked in all the high school yearbooks for that year, but there just wasn't any "Margie" with a short last name listed in any of them.

Stacy knew it was a short last name because when her mother had asked for her court records, the caption of the court documents was headed **Baby Girl ***** with a big black blot over a short (she guessed three letters long) last name. Discouraged, Stacy had gone on other avenues in her search. Without a last name, however, she'd not been able to locate her birth mother.

Stacy was good at helping others search though. One day, Stacy was helping one of the Triad members search through some of the yearbooks from the early 1960s. They were laughing at the clothes and hairstyles in the pages of the book.

"Suddenly," Stacy said, "I was looking at this small shot of the flute section in the band. There was this obviously pregnant student sitting first chair flute, with blonde hair just like mine! Under the photo was a caption listing the people in the photo and she was Margie with a three-letter last name!"

As it was an unusual last name, it didn't take Detective Stacy long to find her birth mother. And she had a bonus. She learned that the birth mother had gone back to her hometown, married her boyfriend, and they had three other children together. Stacy, raised as an only child, had three full siblings and she was going to go meet them all next summer!

Holly Hobbie

I've been doing adoptions long enough that the babies I've placed are starting to look me up. One such instance was a few months ago when Lisa called me. Her mother had reached me several times over the last few years, knowing that I had worked with Lisa's birth mother. Whenever Lisa had had a new question, her mother called me. The last time we'd talked, I told her that I would like to meet Lisa and answer her questions in person. We arranged to meet at a restaurant.

Lisa was bubbly and asked me right off if she looked like her birth mother. Sadly, she did not resemble the woman I remembered. Lisa must have gotten her looks from the birth father's side of the family. I'd only met him on the day he signed the adoption papers, and I didn't remember what he looked like. Lisa asked a lot of questions, good questions that had me remembering more than I thought I could recall.

Lisa told me that at one point her mother had written Arizona Children's Home and received background information. They learned that her birth mother's name was Elizabeth, which they thought was interesting, because Lisa is a diminutive of Elizabeth.

Her adoptive mother had always wondered about the gift that had come with Lisa. In addition to a blanket, there was a Holly Hobbie doll, a character doll popular in the early 1970s. Holly Hobbie wore a long dress with a pinafore and a bonnet. Lisa's adoptive parents had said they only wanted a baby girl and had already decorated the nursery in Holly Hobbie decor. How could this young birth mother have known it? She didn't, of course, but it did tell them that Lisa was meant to be their baby.

Nick

It was Friday night, and too late for the call to be a telemarketer. Yet, when the youthful male voice asked for me by name, I thought he was going to pitch some product I didn't want. I was about to be rude to this young man for calling me after nine-thirty at night, when he said, "My mom told me to call you. You placed me for adoption eighteen years ago. I want to find my birth mother, and my mom says maybe you can help me." That got my attention!

Indeed, I did remember Nick, and especially his birth mother, Maureen. I had thought of him often in the years since he went to live with Gary and Yvette, and I had wondered how he and his little brother, a half brother by blood, had turned out. I didn't hesitate to set an appointment to meet with Nick on the following Sunday at the food court at the local mall.

Lucky for us, Nick brought his mom. I was wondering how I was going to recognize a child I hadn't seen in fifteen years. "There she is," I heard a once-familiar voice say. We decided to go to a sit-down restaurant where we could talk.

Before long, I was recalling how comfortable I felt in Yvette's presence, listening to her New Mexico accent strongly influenced by her husband's Oklahoma twang in the twenty-five years they've been together. Yvette's accent sounds like "home" to this native of west Texas!

When he turned eighteen, Nick explained, he contacted Arizona Children's Home in Tucson and told them he wanted his file. He wanted to know if I had heard from her or knew where she lived.

In the report, he had read how Maureen had worked with me during her pregnancy, but toward the end, before he was born, she met a man named Dominic but called Nick (I had forgotten this detail!) and decided to keep the baby. When he was four months old, she and Nick had fought and she had brought the baby to me for an adoption placement.

With my memory refreshed, I recalled going to visit Gary and Yvette while Nick (called Tony by Maureen) was in foster care. The purpose of my visit was to evaluate whether they would be comfortable taking a four-month-old child instead of a newborn.

I still remember Yvette opening the drawers on the chest that Gary had made by hand, and showing me little T-shirts in size 00. I thought, "Well, he'll never wear those!" The baby already weighed over fifteen pounds. I also met Yvette's mom that day, and in seeing her Hispanic heritage evident in her features, I knew Nick would be accepted into this family for, at four months, Nick was definitely brown skinned and looked Hispanic like his alleged birth father, whose name we did not know.

Nick is a very good-looking young man with the same quick, easy smile he had as a three-year-old when his younger half brother A.J. came to live with them (which was the last time I had seen him). His brother, though also half-Hispanic we believe, has blond hair and blue eyes and is taller than Nick, his mom reports. A.J. is in high school and quite the lady's man. She showed me photos of both boys.

While we talked, Nick sketched on his mom's take-home box that contained her leftover sandwich, revealing an artistic side. I remembered that Maureen had been a very outgoing, friendly young woman. She could remember any telephone number or social security number or address she'd ever had. I asked if he was good at numbers, too.

Yvette said that one of Nick's teachers had wanted him tested for photographic memory because he could see a sheet of music, play it once, and know how to play it from then on. And math was a good subject for him. Nick had moved to Phoenix after finishing high school in order to go to a commercial art school, and was now working rather than going to school. This was okay with his parents. He needs to find himself before he knows what he wants to do.

Important to Nick's finding himself is the search for his roots. I referred him to Search Triad, a group in the Phoenix area that helps people search, much like the group I mentioned in Tucson that is called Triad. I thought he might find a photo of Maureen in a high school annual if he could research that aspect, although it's a long shot.

In this day of computers, a whole industry has grown around adoption search. Some of these services are costly, but they don't have to be. I have hopes that some people work on it fast and furiously and find their birth parents fast. Others work on it off and on when they feel like it, fearful of what might be lurking around the next corner. Certainly, it is a personal growth issue, and many people find that doing a search helps them learn more about themselves than they'd ever imagined.

Just Having a Name ...

Jonathan, who was placed as a baby, was twelve when his learning disability was diagnosed. His adoptive mother tracked me down and asked a favor. Would I find Jon's birth families and ask a specific question? Jon's doctor wanted to put him on a new medication, but a side effect of the medicine was that it could bring on Tourette's syndrome, if there was a predilection for it. She asked if I could find both birth families and ask if there were any incidents of tics or repetitive motion evident in any family members.

It didn't take me long to find Jon's paternal birth grandfather. I learned from him that his son was now married and living in California. I told him why I was calling and asked if there were any unusual movements that people in his family made. He couldn't recall any.

Then I started looking for the birth mother. I was happy to have an excuse to look for her. Sixteen-year-old Lydia had challenged me and the staff of Merilac Lodge where she stayed during her pregnancy. An adopted child herself, placed by the state at the age of three into a family with three boys who wanted a girl to 'round out their family', she was told from the time she was small that she was different.

"Of course, your brothers will go to college," she was told. "But you, you don't have what it takes. You should be content to go to a tech school." She was understandably angry. Her subsequent behavior managed to get her turned back to the state by the time she was twelve. She did, however, maintain contact with her adoptive mother who gave me an address to which I then sent a note.

About a week later I got a call from Lydia. She worked only three miles from my office and we quickly made plans to meet for lunch. "Do you remember how manipulative I was as a teenager?" Did I!

"Well, I found a perfect job for me. I work for a collection agency and I'm good at it! I make good money," said Lydia. I was relieved to learn that she had found her niche.

Over lunch, I learned that Lydia had been even happier to hear from me than I was to hear her voice. "Do you think you could get me some new pictures of the baby?" she asked (until that day she had not known his name was Jonathan). Then she told me that her first husband had destroyed the baby pictures of Jonathan. One day when she came home from work, he told her that the agency had called and said that her child had been killed in a car wreck. This jealous man was so insecure that he couldn't stand for her to have the memory of a child she'd had with another man.

"Oh, Lydia," I said, "you should have called the agency and asked!"

Lydia had more to report. In the intervening years, she'd done a search for her birth parents and had learned that her birth mother and a sister had the same learning disability that we now knew her child had, although Lydia herself does not have it. She was happy she could pass on this updated information.

When I called the adoptive mom to let her know the results of my research, I didn't even give a thought to not calling the birth parents by name. There was a silence at the end of the line. "Did you know their first names?" I asked.

"No," came the soft reply. "And just having a name makes them so much more human." The changes in adoption, I believe, have been positive.

Unexpected End to a Search

I was working at Arizona Children's Home when a private detective came to the agency to see the adoption worker. He explained that he'd been hired by a dying woman in Illinois who wanted to leave her estate to her only surviving relative, a nephew placed for adoption thirty years earlier by her only sister who had since died.

He gave me enough information that I was able to find the cross-reference card by birth date and the woman's sister's last name. I immediately recognized the adoptive family's name, as they owned a widely advertised business in town. What to do next?

We never initiated a search for a child in those days. Common practice at the time was to put the information in the file in case someone from the other side began a search. I went to the agency director for advice. He suggested I contact the adoptive parents and let them decide what they wanted to do about contact.

I reached the adoptive father at his office and explained the reason I was calling. In a sad voice, the man explained that his adopted son Lennie had died at the age of eleven from leukemia. He went on to say that his wife had also died from cancer. I called the private detective and told him I had news of his case that I wanted to tell him in person.

When he arrived at my office, I related the brief information I had gleaned, without revealing the last name. His face turned white. "I think I know the family," he said. "Is it the Rowleski's? We were neighbors! I sat up with them at the hospital when Lennie was dying!

They were with me when my wife died two years later! I moved away and heard that his wife had also passed. I never thought it would be Lennie! I knew he was adopted, but it never occurred to me. . ." He asked to use my phone and then called Mr. Rowleski, and the private detective said he would be right over. They had an old acquaintance to renew.

A month later, the detective called to say that he and the adoptive father had traveled to Chicago with a scrapbook of pictures to share with the dying aunt. Mr. Rowleski was happy to let this woman know of the joy her nephew had brought to his family in his brief life.

PART 6

MIRACLES AND

NEAR MIRACLES

Miracles and Near-Miracles

Some of the people involved in adoptions who are convinced there have been miraculous connections in their lives have shared their stories with me.

A Certain Desk

When I started working on this book, one of my friends whose adoption I was not involved in told me about the special connection she felt when she and her husband got their little girl. Paul and Phyllis were on a business trip in northern Arizona and stayed overnight at a great old hotel in Prescott. This hotel had been refurbished and had mostly antique furniture in the rooms.

Early in the morning of their last day at the hotel, Phyllis received an urgent phone message. Sitting at the oak desk in this room, she learned of her father's death from a heart attack while playing golf in a foreign land. She quickly made plans to join family members in California.

Almost two years later, they made another trip to Prescott and by chance or design stayed in the same room. They had applied to adopt a child from Catholic Social Service (before I worked there) and had been waiting for several months. They'd had "maybe babies" — ones where they were selected by a birth mother who changed her mind after the baby was born.

They were a little discouraged, but Phyllis knew there would be a "right baby" for them. Early on the morning of their last day at the hotel, the phone on the oak desk rang. A friend was calling. "Your caseworker at Catholic Social Service is looking for you and wants you to call her right away. I think this means a baby!" Sitting at the same desk where she had learned of her father's death, Phyllis felt sure he was saying, "This is the baby for you!"

Workers, Unite!

Over the last few years we've had some very good workers in the Flagstaff office of Catholic Social Service. A small office, when you work there you have to cover a lot of miles of Northern Arizona, and as a one-person service, you are both birth parent worker and adoptive parent worker.

Two of our very special workers there have shared the fact that they each placed a baby for adoption. It brings a uniqueness to adoptions work when you are both a role player and a facilitator. Although I knew they were both birth moms, I had not shared that fact with either of them, believing that it was each of their personal stories to share.

Finally they met at a community function and it didn't take them long to share their histories. Kathy, who had recently attended her first conference of American Adoption Congress, a grass roots organization of adoptees and birth parents who are working to change adoption laws in this country, told Julie that she had begun to think of starting a search for her oldest child, who is now in his mid-thirties.

As they shared more of their stories, they learned they had even more in common. Both of these women, in their late teens, had gone to a small town in Pennsylvania where they worked with the same doctor – though it was several years between their events – and had used the same attorney.

What are the chances, they reasoned, that they would both move from the eastern part of the United States to a small town in

Northern Arizona, and then discover they had been to the same doctor and the same attorney at different times? They will certainly be able to share support for searching for their children, if and when they decide to do so.

Amaryllis

An African-American couple had been waiting for a second child through Arizona Children's Home for over a year. One day, the wife called and made an appointment to come in and talk to me. She sounded sad.

When Vivian arrived, she said she was distressed because she was approaching both her fortieth birthday and her twelfth wedding anniversary and the anticipated second child had not yet arrived. She sat on my couch and cried, feeling helpless to control the wait.

I was struck by her sadness and after Vivian left, I called a couple of other agencies to see if they knew of any African-American children needing homes. One call led to another and soon I was speaking to a worker at an agency in Texas.

They had an African-American baby boy born just that morning and they didn't have a family for him. We exchanged information about my family and their baby, and when I called Vivian and Mark, they were ecstatic they could have a baby boy as a brother for their happy little three-year-old girl. Now we had to get approval from Interstate Compact on Placement of Children (ICPC) before the child could leave Texas and come to Arizona.

In Vivian and Mark's case, Texas law required pictures and a floor plan of their house, and proof of liability insurance – additional requirements to what Arizona required. Getting the paperwork through proper channels took longer than we had anticipated. Vivian called one day and said, "Beth, this is like being dilated to ten and nothing's happening!"

Finally we received the word that the paperwork was approved and the social worker from Texas brought the baby to Tucson. I met her and the baby at the airport and Vivian and Mark waited at my office, which was nearby.

Everyone was ecstatic to receive the new baby boy, and the social worker from Texas asked if she could come to the house that afternoon before her flight left and see the baby Jacob in his new home.

After the visit, we two social workers were leaving Mark and Vivian's house when Vivian said, "Did I ever tell you about my sign from God that this was going to happen?"

She proceeded to tell us what happened after she left my office on that day when she was so sad. Vivian now confessed that there were two other issues that had been troubling her that day, issues she'd not shared with me.

Her best friend had recently been diagnosed with a brain tumor and was having surgery to see if it was malignant. And Mark had just had tests run on a growth on his foot.

"After I left your office that day," she explained, "I went home and I prayed and cried all afternoon. I said, 'Lord, send me a sign. I need to know that you hear my prayers.'

The next morning when I got up and came to the kitchen, I looked out on the patio. Someone had given me a gift of a potted plant at Christmas, but nothing had happened to it in spite of watering it every day. I thought it was dying, so I had set it out on the deck a few days earlier. That morning I looked out the window and there were three huge red blossoms. The amaryllis had bloomed. I had my sign from God! And within a few hours, Beth, you called me to tell me about Jacob, my friend's mother called to say her daughter's tumor wasn't cancer, and Mark got a good report from his doctor! My prayers were all answered!"

The other social worker and I both had tears in our eyes as we walked to the car. "Now I know this baby is where he's supposed to be!" said my newfound friend from Texas — Amarillo, Texas, to be precise.

What Are the Odds We'd Meet?

Speaking of Amarillo, this next story isn't about adoption, but it's something I experienced at a national conference on adoptions. It's so serendipitous, it belongs in this book.

There was something hauntingly familiar about the tall thin man who was introduced as being from an agency in Dallas. I finally decided the familiarity was because his accent was the same as the region I grew up in, in West Texas. When we were seated at the same round table at the next breakfast, I asked the inevitable: "Where were you raised?"

His answer was, "My father was a Methodist minister, so we lived in several small towns on the Texas Plains. Mostly I grew up in Lorenzo," he said, naming a town of less than 1500. "You're kidding," I said, "If you're from Lorenzo, then you would know Floydada, where I went to high school."

"Well, then, if you know Floydada, where I'm really from is Cone!" We laughed. Cone is a small community that in my youth was centered around a cotton gin, a school building, a Baptist church and a Methodist church that, incredulously, was "on a circuit" with the small Methodist church where I'd grown up: in Harmony, an even smaller community west of Cone.

We'd even "shared preachers" with Cone when I was small, the minister at our church on the second and fourth Sundays and at Cone on the first and third; any month with a fifth Sunday would find morning services at Cone and evening services at Carr's Chapel.

Cone was the larger of the two congregations. They supplied a parsonage, where the minister and his family could live. "What years were you at Cone?" I wanted to know. It was after I had grown up and left for school, and after our two congregations no longer shared a preacher. "Did you live there? In the parsonage?"

He had been too small to have memories of Cone, but he knew they lived at Cone before they moved to Lorenzo.

My family had donated the house that became that parsonage when they built a new house, I told him. I remembered "our house" being moved by truck – long before such a sight as a house moving down the highway on a trailer was common when I was six.

This adoptions worker from Texas and I, an adoptions worker from Arizona, shared the most basic of environments: the first house we'd each lived in!

A Christmas Robin

One of the changes that came with openness is that we have encouraged waiting adoptive couples to network to find a baby on their own. It can be empowering for infertile couples who have felt that everything has been out of their control to start talking to friends and family about their adoption hopes and plans.

One of the couples who talked to their friends at work was Ron and Beverly. Ron worked at the Veteran's Hospital, and one of the young doctors who was on intern rotation, left the Veterans Administration for an outpost in Bullhead City on the Colorado River in western Arizona.

On the last day of his rotation there, Friday, December 21, the doctor called Ron and Beverly. He was excited as he told them that he'd just delivered a baby girl and the mother wanted to place her for adoption. "I told her all about you," their friend said. "She says that she wants you to take the baby!"

As I said, it was Friday, and the beginning of Christmas vacation. Their adoption worker had left on vacation on the same day. Ron and Beverly didn't even have my phone number, but somehow they found me and called about eight-thirty that evening. I was soon on the phone talking to the doctor, and then the birth mother, who confirmed that she wished to place the baby for adoption.

In those days, Bullhead City's hospital wasn't equipped for deliveries. She had come in fully dilated, however, and there had been no time to get her to Kingman, the closest hospital that did deliveries in those days. Hospital staff in Bullhead City called for a helicopter, but the winter winds were blowing too hard for a helicopter to negotiate the mountainous terrain in the Colorado River valley. Now they were waiting for an ambulance to drive mother and baby to the hospital in Kingman. I promised to call her the next day, and see how she felt about her decision.

Over the next two days, I spoke on the phone daily with this young woman who worked at one of the casinos across the river in Laughlin, Nevada. No one knew of her pregnancy, and she preferred to keep it that way. I got enough information that I could fill out the adoption papers, and made plans to drive over to the Colorado River valley on Christmas Eve. Kingman's hospital would keep the baby till then.

Laughlin is a lonely place to spend Christmas Eve, but the hotel rates are inexpensive! I arrived on the twenty-third of December. I would take consents on Christmas Eve, but tonight we would meet and fill out background papers. I met the birth mother as arranged, and the next morning we met at the Bullhead City Hospital where she had delivered so that the doctor who had arranged this match could be a witness to the papers she would sign.

If he had not been on duty, if he had not heard Ron's plea to keep an open eye, Ron and Beverly would not have had this baby. Surely, this was meant to be.

On Christmas Eve, then, with signed adoption consents, I drove to Kingman and picked up the baby girl, who Ron and Beverly would name Robin.

Placing a baby on Christmas Eve is neat!

A Girl with Blue Eyes

Most of the placements I've worked with through the years have been newborns just a few days old. Occasionally, we've had children as old as three or four.

An older child may be a case in which birth grandparents are raising a child and eventually feel the need to have a younger couple assume the responsibilities of parenting. Or it may be that a child has been raised by a young birth mother for whom the romanticism of motherhood came to a screeching halt.

Single parenting is very difficult. The most common remark I hear from new adoptive parents on a first home visit after placement is: "I have a new respect for single moms. I don't know how they do it. This takes at least two people!"

One spring day, I had a call from a woman whose oldest daughter, at sixteen, had had a baby girl. The infant was now was twenty months old and her daughter was thinking of making an adoption plan for her baby.

When I met with Natalie, a beautiful young woman about to turn eighteen, she told me: "I don't want you to think that I'm doing this because I want a new life for myself. It's not about me. I'm only doing this because I want her to have more than I can give her. I want her to have both a mommy and a daddy. I want her to be able to go to college. I want her to be able to follow her dream."

Kenna was a darling little girl with blonde ringlets and big blue eyes. She played quietly at our feet while we talked. I explained to Natalie that we had to make contact with the birth father and be sure that he would agree with the plan, or at the very least not interfere. Natalie gave me his address and work schedule. I wasn't worried about Kenna being able to make a transition to a new home. Although there had been a constant flow of different roommates in her short bout with independence, Natalie had always been Kenna's mommy. I promised to gather some profiles of adoptive parents for her to consider the next time we met.

Back at the office, we looked through our book of waiting families. There was one couple who had waited the longest. Tom and Kathy, who already had a son they'd adopted four years earlier, had waited longer than most because they really wanted a healthy Caucasian baby girl whose mother had taken no drugs or alcohol. I doubted they would take a girl almost two years old, but we decided to ask.

Kathy's immediate response was one of acceptance for this little girl. "I was just going to call and ask if you ever got older kids. Last week, I met a little girl at McDonald's. She was eight years old and had been living with her grandmother. She told me she was going to get a new mommy and daddy and my heart went out to her. I said to Tom, 'Why couldn't we adopt her?' It got me to thinking about a child who might need us that wouldn't be a baby." I gave her the details about Kenna's birth so she could call her husband at work and see if he would agree to have their profile shown to Natalie.

I later learned that when she told him the birth date, Tom blurted out, "Oh, my God! Kathy, she was born on the same day that Mom died!"

And then Kathy told me that when she knew she was dying of cancer, Tom's mom had turned to them and said, "I'm going to Heaven and ask God to send you a blue-eyed little girl!"

Protected by Angels

When I interviewed Hollis at the hospital the day Jesse was born, she was polite, but not very forthcoming with the details of her life. She answered my questions about her health history, her personal life, and her social situation with short but sufficient answers. Then I asked about the father of the baby.

"His name is Todd, but he's believed to be dead," she said. When I pressed for more details she responded tersely, "I don't want to talk about it." With that, she doubled over with abdominal cramps.

Abdominal cramps twelve hours after delivery, even a baby that's born a month early, aren't all that unusual. Still, I suspected these might be drug withdrawals, because the hospital's social worker, when I arrived at the hospital, said that Hollis had admitted using cocaine on a daily basis all through the pregnancy.

When I asked if she had concerns about any of a host of personal-choice items (*e.g.*, relationships, alcohol and/or drug abuse), she said, "I don't have a problem with drugs. As a matter of fact, I like my drugs. My goal is to get high and stay that way. That's why I'm not cut out to be a mother. I need my drugs more than I need a baby."

We discussed families for the baby to grow up with and she requested a Catholic family, one without previous children. From the family profiles I had brought with me, she selected her favorite. Then I went to visit the baby in the nursery.

Underweight and bony, he appeared jittery in the harsh light of the hospital's nursery. He had a high-pitched cry, an extreme startle reflex, and was under an oxygen hood to help regulate his elevated heart rate.

The staff at the hospital had heard this was an adoption. One of the nurses expressed skepticism about adoptive parents being able to understand the special needs of a child born with drugs in his system.

Hollis stayed in the hospital just long enough to sign the papers necessary for the baby to go with the agency upon hospital discharge. Under Arizona law, the earliest the adoption papers could be signed was seventy-two hours after the birth. Since I hadn't met her before delivery, I had suggested she take more than the required three-day period to make a final choice. We had made an appointment for her to meet me at my office the following Monday — six days after the birth.

I knew the family she had picked out would say yes. I had done their home study and remembered Theresa saying that she would take a baby with intrauterine drug exposure, even a baby that was HIV positive. I called her and gave her details of the baby's birth. She and her husband agreed to meet me at the hospital that evening to see the baby and decide if they would take him home or request he go into a neutral home until the adoption papers were signed.

As I drove to the hospital, I thought of the stationery Theresa and Jim had chosen for their "Dear Birth Parent" letter. It had Raphaelite cherubs across the bottom of the page. Theresa was an avid collector of angel pictures. They'd even bought a house because there was a sticker in the window that read, "This house is protected by Angels." It turned out to be the logo of a defunct alarm company, but the decal had stayed because it won Theresa's heart.

When I walked into the hospital and passed the nurse's station, someone had propped up a thank-you card from a previous new mother. The card was decorated with the exact same angels as those on Theresa and Jim's stationery. This was a good sign. Jim and Theresa visited the baby and decided to take him home with them upon discharge rather than have him go into a receiving home.

Hollis kept her appointment with me the next Monday, but asked to take the adoption papers home with her. "I figure that anything I read while flat on my back deserves my undivided attention," she explained.

She appeared to be stable and not under the influence of narcotics that day. Still, I asked her to please not do any drugs for at least twelve hours prior to the scheduled time the next day when we were to take consents.

I told her of the baby's condition and of the prospective adoptive family's acceptance of the baby and their taking him home as soon as he was discharged from the hospital. I even told her about the angels on the card at the hospital and how they were the same as the angels on Theresa and Jim's stationery. Hollis remained stoic, but agreed to meet with Theresa and Jim the next day when she came to sign papers.

I never saw Hollis again. She missed her appointment. She did respond to a telephone message I left and set another appointment but she didn't keep that one either. I continued to write letters and leave phone messages, but got no reply.

I had our private detective go with me to her address. The person who answered the door said Hollis was out of town but expected later in the day. We left a message for her there, too. Still, I heard nothing from Hollis. Under a new law in Arizona, we could terminate her rights under abandonment at three months. We prepared to do so.

A week before the three-month deadline, I was paged by our receptionist and told there was someone at the front desk asking to see me. "It's an emergency," she added.

Wanda, a tall woman with long blonde hair, told me she had been a friend of Hollis's for ten years and had spent the last week with her at the hospital. Just two days before, Hollis had died from a cocaine overdose. Hollis's mother had already arrived from another state to see to her daughter's funeral arrangements and together they had discovered the unsigned adoption papers.

Although Wanda had known Hollis was pregnant, her mother had not. Wanda asked if the baby was in foster care. She wanted to know if she could adopt the baby. She assured me that Hollis's mother was in agreement. As soon as I described the family who had taken Jesse home from the hospital, Wanda backed off. "I could never destroy a family who has been loving him for three months!" she said.

"Now what?" I asked our agency's attorney who had prepared the abandonment and termination paperwork. I was told that we'd only need a death certificate, as Hollis's signature on the hospital release agreement indicated intent to place the baby for adoption.

When Hollis's mother sent the death certificate, we also got photocopies from Hollis's high school senior yearbook, to pass on to the adoptive parents. Hollis, a bright and pretty girl in high school, had been active on the debate team, in the National Honor Society, and on the school's quiz team. At that time, her mom said, Hollis had planned to be an attorney and would have made a good one. Drugs had ended her dreams and those of her parents for their daughter's future.

A week later, the private detective who had helped me search for Hollis and the birth father called me with additional news. He was writing up his Affidavit of Due Diligence to let the court know of his efforts to locate the father when he ran a computer check and found Todd in prison in a distant county.

I knew I had to write him now, but I called our attorney and asked her if I had to tell him of Hollis's death. "Not unless he asks," she said. "But don't lie to him if he does." I wrote Todd a letter explaining that Hollis had named him as the father of a baby boy who had been born three months earlier and that he was in a potential adoptive home. I enclosed adoption papers and background forms for him to fill out and invited his participation in his baby's future. I breathed a prayer for understanding as I mailed these papers off to him.

The other staff members and I felt helpless, but we still wanted to do something more for Hollis. Because she was Catholic and had requested a Catholic family for her baby, we asked that a Mass be said in her honor. Several of our staff attended, as did the adoptive mother. It gave everyone solace. Theresa told me later that as she sat in the church, she prayed, "Please, Hollis, find Todd and let him sign the adoption papers."

That afternoon, I got a call from Todd. He'd received my letter and he said it was the first that he'd known about the baby. Since he was in no way able to take care of a baby at this point in his life, he agreed to sign the papers to allow the baby to be adopted. He asked how the baby was doing, and I reported the baby was doing well. And then he asked about Hollis. When I hesitated, he asked, "Is she okay?" I took a deep breath and told him that she had died of a drug overdose just three months after the baby was born. It was a hard blow for him.

Shortly after that call, I received a heartfelt letter from him accompanied by his notarized consents and background forms. Realizing the death would be difficult for him to accept, I sent him a copy of the death certificate, and for several months we were pen pals as he worked through his sadness. In his subsequent letters, he revealed a "whole person" who had built sets for a movie and worked on race cars. Mechanical interests run in both baby Jesse's families. Hollis's father wrote that he has an old Corvette, which he has lovingly restored. And the adoptive father Jim earns his living as an airplane mechanic and works on cars in his spare time.

Jim and Theresa have written to Jesse's grandparents and to Todd, requesting photos for the scrapbook they're putting together for Jesse. The open adoption which they originally planned with unseen birth parents now has turned into letters and pictures and visits with extended family members. The irony is that we've got far more family history since her death than Hollis ever shared with me in the hospital. Hollis's mother plans to come to Phoenix to meet little Jesse and his parents. The adopting parents welcome the inclusion of Hollis's parents into their extended family.

And the angels continue to smile! Hanging in my office is a framed petit point embroidered picture entitled "Angel of the Sea" that was given to me by Theresa. It shows a beautiful angel with yellow hair holding an infant. There are swirls of teal and blue around the angel's robe, and gold threads and tiny pearls stitched onto it.

Theresa began working on this project while waiting for the call that she and her husband would be getting a baby. She intended to give it to the birth mother of the child they would some day adopt. When they learned of Hollis's death, she asked if I would take it. I knew just where in my office I would put it, and I often tell the story of the angel that brought Jesse.

Theresa and Jim chose the name Jesse for Hollis's baby boy. Months later, they looked up the name online and learned that the meaning for Jesse is "the gift." Although little Jesse had a rough start, he is now healthy and happy and truly a gift to everyone.

An Amazing Angels Update

A family get-together was planned for my office around Christmastime the Christmas after Jesse's birth. Nine-month-old Jesse would be meeting his birth grandmother Janet and her husband Bob who had come from New England to Phoenix for the holidays. Jim and Theresa, Jesse's new parents, couldn't help but be anxious about meeting Janet and Bob.

Initially, Theresa had been afraid that Janet would want to take her only child's son to raise. Janet supported the adoption, but Jim and Theresa needed to hear those words directly from her. Once they were assured, they eagerly shared information about Jesse and how he had influenced all their family in a positive way. Bob and Janet shared more of Hollis's family history.

Christmas presents were exchanged. Bob and Janet had brought Jesse a soft teddy bear, and Jim and Theresa gave the grandparents framed photographs of Jesse, including the just-selected Christmas shots. The picture of Jesse's round little smiling face framed with abundant blond hair under a Santa hat charmed us all. By the end of the gathering, he was willingly allowing Janet to hold and feed him, as long as Mommy was in sight! He obviously enjoyed being the center of attention.

Bill, Janet's former husband and Hollis's dad, had sent a Christmas present to my office. In a separate card, Bill had written me that he was sending "a tiger for a tiger." The box had arrived two days earlier from Massachusetts and had been sitting in my office.

I brought the box in and Jim began unwrapping the package. Jesse was fussing, and Jim turned to help. I picked up the scissors and split the seal of the tape on the bottom of the box because it looked easier to open, having just one layer of tape when the top had several layers of tape holding it together. As I parted the bottom flaps of the cardboard box, a maize-colored business card caught my eye. I pulled it out and was stunned to read the following words written on the back of the business card:

Hi Mom. Merry Xmas from Phoenix.

I hope you are keeping warm.

Please say Hi to Bob for me. Love, Hollis

Somewhat shaken, I handed the card to Janet. We examined the box and discovered an old mailing label addressed to Janet. She remembered that Hollis had sent a cactus in it from Phoenix four years earlier.

Now the box had been used by Bill to send Jesse his Christmas present. This card, never seen before by her parents, had worked its way to the bottom of the box and been stuck in between the box flaps for four years!

We all agreed that Hollis had found a way to tell us all that she approved of our meeting!

The Believer

Wanda was single when she adopted. As she explained it, her need to be a mother was stronger than her need for a partner. In the end, as you will see, she got both.

Wanda delights in telling others how she was at a book fair at her local community college when the person manning the booth asked her, "Are you a believer?" When Wanda replied in the affirmative, he told her he was moved to share with her this story, although he didn't know exactly why.

"At our church," he said earnestly, "we are praying for a couple in our congregation. They have a daughter who is ill and pregnant. She also has an eleven-year-old girl who is being raised by her husband's parents, but they feel they are too old to care for a second child." Wanda told him that she would add this family to her prayers. Then he invited her to come to his home for a Bible study and prayer group that evening and she decided to go.

Wanda had just enrolled in training classes to become a foster family for "older children" who needed safe homes to grow up in. As she thought back over her conversation with the man, she thought he'd meant that the grandparents could no longer care for the eleven-year-old. She wondered whether she might be the right person to raise this older child.

At the man's house later that day, Wanda thought that the birth mother might be there. She looked around but didn't see anyone who was pregnant. In fact, most of the people there were older than Wanda. After the meeting, she was finally introduced to the parents whose daughter was in the prayers of this congregation. It was the child the daughter was carrying that needed a home.

The paternal grandparents who were raising the eleven-year-old were doubtful that any single woman could handle raising a child on her own. Somewhat reluctantly, they agreed to come to my office to meet Wanda.

Wanda prepared a book to tell them about her life and how she'd lived in several countries and served as a missionary. She had once been a foster parent on the Navajo reservation. That experience, she said, taught her she wanted children in her life in a permanent way.

Wanda's soft Scottish brogue and long red ponytail won over the heart of the very Scottish Mr. Campbell. Wanda held her own in the conversation in which they shared their personal opinions on the different Scottish clans and their particular patterns. She really knew her stuff!

Esther, the pregnant birth mother, sat quietly without saying a word. The office visit ended with Wanda inviting the family to come to her home. As they got into the car, Esther asked Wanda, "Do you want to adopt my baby?" Wanda told her tearfully that she would love to have the opportunity to do so.

"I think that would be fine," said Esther.

Wanda did adopt Esther's baby. Wanda had once been engaged to a wonderful man, but as the divorced father of teenagers whose demands were especially wearing at the time, he told Wanda he didn't want kids. He'd already done "the daddy thing" and had no desire to repeat it.

Then the baby Wanda adopted won him over! So when the baby was six months old, they decorated her stroller and pushed it down the aisle at their wedding. When they've been married for a year, they will participate in a stepparent adoption.

A Special Parting

In 1999, I attended two memorial services for birth mothers. The first was for Hollis, and the second was for Esther. Just five months after the birth of her daughter Cassandra, who was placed for adoption, Esther, Cassandra's first mother, was diagnosed with leukemia and given just a few months to live. She chose not to undergo radiation treatment.

I sat amongst her parents' friends from their church congregation and listened to the family recall special memories of their daughter Esther. They were recollections of a different Esther than the one I'd met. This was the Esther before she had schizophrenia; Esther when she was a cheerleader; Esther when she participated in piano recitals; Esther who wrote a hymn that her family sang today, a hymn in praise of her Heavenly Father.

I knew this was a unique experience, for recognized in the memorial's program was the adoptive family, Wanda and Mark and Esther's baby Cassandra. They sat with the family, united in their grief.

Not many adoptive and birth families of the olden days — the days of secrecy in adoption — ever had the chance to participate in such meaningful family rituals.

Yes, I believe that the changes in adoption are good.

Afterword

From time to time in my years of adoptions work, I have told one or another of these stories to illustrate a point. In 1993, when adoption was getting a particularly black eye in the media with the Baby Jessica and Baby Richard cases, I joined Toastmasters to hone my public speaking skills. In my speeches, I told several positive stories about adoption. I found a willing audience outside the realm of adoption, and that was the germination of a plan to write this book.

In adoption education classes and in birth parent support groups, I'm always telling adoption participants that they have a new role, which is to become educators of the general public about adoption issues so that their children will find more acceptance. Whenever I speak to a non-adoption audience (like a high school class) someone always comes up and tells me, "I am adopted (or my boyfriend or my cousin is), and this is the first time I've heard something positive about adoption (or about birth mothers)."

One person who read an early draft of my book said, "You've left out an important part of your story. How did participating in these adoption events shape your life?"

How *did* my adoption work affect my life? Answering the question from my childhood personae, I would tell it this way: I learned to trust God; to trust that He answers prayers. But my concept of God has expanded over the years.

I now say it is a Trust in the Universe. There are many paths to find God, and many names for God. I believe every person is responsible for finding their own path, and I accept that there are many paths that lead to the same ideal – no matter what we each call it. I have been honored to play a part in building families.

Acknowledgements

While I've used the editorial "we" and "our agency" in these stories, I want to give a special thanks to the administrators who've given me the opportunity to work in this wonderful arena: Arizona Children's Home Association, Tucson: Arthur Elrey, Julius Modlinski, Rick Rikkers, Fred Chaffee; Southwest Adoption Center, Inc.: Mike Sullivan, Jim Medlock; Arizona Children's Home Association, Phoenix: Terry Hartman, Sharon Elrod; Family Service Agency, Phoenix: Jane Hartman, Brenda Fleming; Hand in Hand International, Phoenix: Margot Reinhart, Marilee Lane; Casey Family Program, Phoenix: Beth Kuhn; Catholic Social Service, Phoenix: Connie Mitchell, Maureen Webster, Scott Palluck, Susan Brenchley, Diane Ellis, Kristen Schmidt and Paul Martodam.

The camaraderie of my co-workers has been a great source of emotional support and learning. These include Helen Tisher, Joan Schumann, Anita Wooten, Marcie Velen, Janet Dews, Janis Scott, Gloria Halle; Jane Daniel, Mary LeBraun, Lexann Downey-Lewis, Sister Mary Ann Bogosoff; JoAnn Blevins, Gloria Dayley, J'Ann Pope, Beverly Quidort; Chris Richert, Joan Allen, Mike White, Christie Powell, Phyllis Habib; Shirley Pusey; Carol Carpenter, Sheryl Baker, Jean Sokol, Colleen Junck, Virginia Hout, Kearstin Switzenberg Nuckols, Carrie Mascaro, Kathy Raynes, Adrienne

Kraft, Melissa Noriega-Poure, Rebecca Van Wagenen Bermudez, MacKenzie VanWormer, Tracy Anderson and Vivian Schwabish.

I've had great support from the secretaries and administrative assistants and other support staff who have kept us running: Mary Gustafson, Stephanie Downey, Linda Snyder, Don Dugdale; Judy Gorter, Mary Wendt, Mary Kate Roberts, Dawn Johnson; Dot Latham; Wanda Chauklin, Diana Singer, Barb Graham and Beverly Elias.

Along the way various attorneys have lent their knowledge and helped me understand the legal ramifications of adoption: Mary Mangotich, Mike Sullivan, Kelly Sifferman, Kathryn Pidgeon, Mary Verdier, Rita Meiser and Jay McCarthy.

One very special group of people without whom this book could not have been written is the foster parents who keep babies during the indefinite time period when a child needs a place to stay. Their willingness to be on-call for the very personal and selfless care needed for an infant who hasn't learned yet how to socialize has made a silent difference in many a life. Foster parents/receiving home parents I've worked with include Leonard and Dolores Hartman, Tom and Susan Butler, Gary and Debbie Lucken, Gary and Nancy Rogers, Mike and Karen Ryan, Steve and Anita Wilson, Arnold and Phyllis Moore, and Kevin and Julia Cleary.

And a special thanks goes to these people who helped me on this book: Linda Radke of Five Star Publishing; Paul M. Howey, who helped me sort through the ideas; Diana Singer, who helped iron out the syntax, plus many friends and reviewers. I carried this book around for more than ten years. It was Laura Orsini who has a business helping people self-publish their books who tells me my voice is needed. Laura is also a birth mother. That photo that appears on the cover is by Samantha Wood Photography. Eduardo Cervino and Lesley Sudders were invaluable in helping to shape up the actual book. Boy! I could not have made it without them!

Finally, I want to thank the many families who have shared their hearts, their dreams and their stories through the years, in all of the stories I've told and those I've not yet told. For those whose stories aren't here, there's still time for more.

About the Author

Beth Kozan worked for adoption agencies in Tucson, Scottsdale and Phoenix Arizona from 1979 to 2008. She retired from adoption agency work and opened a private practice for adoption counseling, and to write books. Adoption: More Than By Chance is her first book, and she is writing her second book, Helping the Birth Mother You Know.

Beth grew up in a small agricultural community in Texas where she enjoyed the support of a loving community and excellent schools. Future books will reflect the importance of building communities of support.